CONTENTS

Disclaimer

All content reflects the author's opinions and should not be misconstrued for professional investment or tax advice. The views reflected are informational in nature, and in no way predict or ensure any specific outcome. Investing in the stock market involves risk and you can lose money, please do your own thorough research before investing. This book is not endorsed, approved, nor recommended by any public or private financial institution.

Foreword

"Beware the investment activity that produces applause; the great moves are usually greeted by yawns." -Warren Buffet. This book is not a get-rich-quick scheme, it is a get-rich-slow investing template. I almost never wrote this book. I am an introvert by nature and tend to shy away from the spotlight including social media, I like to live a private life. It took me years of trial and error making many mistakes along the way, to learn how to invest in the stock market confidently and successfully. A part of me wanted to quietly work my plan and keep to myself. That is the safest, after all, to never put oneself out there for criticism and critique.

But these ideas have been rattling around my head for over 8 years, and when I got sick for a few weeks I kept thinking, (as one does with way too much time to think while sick), what if something serious happened to me? My wife and young kids, friends and extended family, and everyone else in the investing and personal finance community who might care to learn what I have learned, would be clueless to the investing strategies and unique system I've developed. What a waste.

As I read and learned over the years, I gleaned many brilliant nuggets of stock market investing knowledge from so many smart men and women. However, I grew increasingly frustrated that I didn't have a good single resource to put it all together into a workable investing format. So, I created one.

Ultimately, I decided to get out of my shell and share what I have learned with the world. Every principle of this book may not apply or appeal to everyone, but I believe everyone can learn something, hopefully many things, about a different way to think about investing. It's not that I have it all figured out, far from it, but investing is nearly all I've thought about for years. I've developed the unique Stock Planting [TM] approach as a result of all this thinking and tinkering with many different investing ideas and strategies. It is a series of tactical steps incorporated with an understanding of how investors typically think and act, and how to avoid some of the emotional pitfalls of investing.

Instead of giving specific companies' stock as recommendations to buy, I want to teach you to build your own investing system, to plant the simple seeds that could help power potentially transformational wealth for you in the future. After building a financial foundation, I want to teach you how to choose your own stocks, with seed-like tiny positions at first, that can grow over time as you grow in your knowledge and confidence in investing. You will learn to add to some of these growing seed-like positions in a methodical and unique manner. Eventually, you will learn to harvest (sell) some fully grown stock positions when your personalized system dictates. No greed, no fear, no panic; instead, a systematized calm.

Introduction

As a young teenager I worked on a potato farm for a couple of summers and each fall harvest. I still remember squelching through the mud, moving sprinkler lines by hand, carefully stepping over the rows of potatoes peeking their new stems and leaves through the dirt. Yes, per the assumed potato stereotype, it was an Idaho farm. The process of farming was mostly unhurried throughout the year, with a few weeks sprint for the harvest at the end of the season. The physical work was demanding, and the measured pace and care for the plants that meant the farms' future payday, was fulfilling. The work required planning, patience, nurturing, and a little bit of luck with sporadic rain showers to get a great crop. So it is, with investing.

I am an inherently optimistic person, sprinkled in with some skepticism and practicality. I believe financial freedom and wealth-building are available to everyone. I believe over time, although there are many terrible things that happen in the world and will unfortunately continue to happen, to borrow a line from David Gardner, *Rule Breaker Investing* podcast host, "The good guys still outnumber the bad."

I believe there are so many good, hard-working people in many innovative companies, industries, and countries around the world that are constantly adapting to the changing marketplaces around them. Because of this ability to adapt, I believe over the long term the world will keep improving, therefore over extended periods of time, the stock market will go up.

Those good companies and people are worth investing in, as are you. I have found that many people and companies are, by and large, terrible at predicting short term future outcomes, but wonderfully resourceful at adapting to change. When a person decides to change some aspect of their life for the better, It can take time for the results to show on the outside to others.

Similarly, it can take time for a company's positive decisions for adaptation and change to be reflected in its earnings and stock price.

The U.S stock market has never declined over any 20-year period. While rare, there are 10-year periods where it has. Close in on 5, 3, and 1-year stretches, and the number of years where the stock market has declined increases. This is one reason investing can be so difficult for many. But I hope hearing this can help you understand why patience and long holding periods in the market can help ease fears about market declines. Taking the multi-year approach can also let winning companies prove themselves worthy of your investing dollars over longer measuring periods.

As mentioned in the foreword, I wrote this book because while I have found so many investing gems within many books written by brilliant men and women, I never found a book that tied it all together. There are some that focus on building a financial foundation, yet falter a bit in the later, tactical steps of investing in the stock market. There are others that focus very well on topics such as investing behavior, long-term stock market returns, how it is hard to beat the market and why you shouldn't try, etc. There are even some which focus a great deal on stock picking and deep market and company analysis, yet brush by the foundational aspects of who should invest, and in what life phase it might make the most sense to varying readers.

I wanted this book to be a connecting thread from many smart people who I will quote throughout the book, as well as my own thoughts and experiences. I want to give you a new framework and system to improve your own financial journey, by following some or all of these principles. I have come to realize that investing isn't really that hard once you piece it all together, but it can be overwhelming if you don't know where to begin, or if you try to rush into specific aspects of investing without seeing the bigger picture.

No one gets the same starting line in life, which, unfortunately, makes life inherently not fair. I wish that were not the case, but I want to help build your confidence in your ability to win financially. Wherever you are, by taking a longer-term financial view of your life and implementing a few simple (though behaviorally likely very challenging) steps, I'm going to teach you how to set a baseline financial foundation for your life, no matter where you are starting today. Setting up the foundation portion will take everyone varying amounts of time, but once you're there, I want to teach you how to set up your own personalized investing system in a simple way that will be unique to you, your risk tolerances, and your time horizon.

I am an avid reader, and love learning from people more knowledgeable than me in various subjects. I don't dwell on the past and am always forward-thinking, and truthfully sometimes have a hard time staying in the present because my mind is always on future possibilities. I think this is why stock market investing appeals to me so much. It requires a large dose of optimism about the future and an even larger dose of patience, two things which I feel fortunate to have in abundance.

I have read hundreds if not thousands of books over my lifetime, and that is not an exaggeration. Starting young it was teen sleuth mysteries and as I got into my teenage years it shifted into all sorts of classic literature, philosophy, self-help, business and leadership, fantasy, and sci-fi novel series; I read everything I could get my hands on. Over the past 7 years I took that passion for learning and reading into personal finance and investing.

Hearing the many different stories of those who accumulated wealth during their lifetimes, I wanted to learn how everyone got all this money. Where did it come from? What did they do to achieve it? Over time I realized that although some had sold businesses for large payouts or built real estate empires, many had accumulated their wealth through steady and consistent investing in the stock market, often through retirement plans.

The secret, it seemed, was a lot more boring than I thought. Successful investors had lived decades longer than me, allowing compound interest to work in their favor and had been consistent in at least two aspects of their financial lives. Living below their means enough to contribute to investment accounts regularly, and having the emotional fortitude not to panic and leave the market entirely during down markets. The key here was their time invested in the market. I, as a 27-year-old at the time, was unjustly comparing my own meager barely positive net worth to others that had been investing since before I was born.

There has been a lot of noise and discussion about investing over the decades, especially in the financial media. Most people don't think about investing, or try not to think about it, until they hear on the news that the market has suffered some large drop for this or that reason.

I heard on a podcast once with psychologist Morgan Housel about a fascinating phenomenon. Our brains do a weird thing called "extreme discounting", where when we hear of a short-term negative event in a company, the economy, or the geopolitical sphere, we extrapolate that event forward out to the near and even distant future. This can cause us to make knee-jerk decisions. This is very common with investors in the stock market. It causes some to sell a stock, or sell all stocks they own, and wait in cash for some recovery.

There is often no logical rationale for the extent of this extreme discounting reaction, but it affects millions of people, often without them realizing it. You hear a particularly bad bit of news from a company and your brain instantly makes judgments about how that otherwise profitable and thriving company's stock must be headed to zero, through a spiraling thought-pattern that you would have trouble describing to someone else later. Or, you hear a bad bit of news on the international stage, and imagine the demise of the stock market as we know it, so you sell everything you had invested in, especially because friends and neighbors might be doing the same thing. We are emotional creatures trying to be logical most of the time. We can have robust charts, statistics, all sorts of useful information at hand. Yet in times of perceived threat or panic the urge to "do something" is often the go-to reaction, and the effect of this reaction usually causes us longer-term financial pain even if it alleviates that short-term itch to act.

In addition to an investing system, I would like to introduce you to some strategies that could help you reduce that fear and pay attention just enough to be a steady, consistent participant in the stock market, permitting you to create wonderful wealth if you can stick with it.

As mentioned in the foreword, this is no get-rich-quick scheme. In fact, if done right, it will take decades and be primarily dull, punctuated by rare moments of brief excitement. What a compelling introduction, right? Why continue reading? Here's why. By the end of this book, we will have built a solid foundation of knowledge about what investing is, why everyone should do it, what life adjustments could be made now to help get you ready to invest, and what tax considerations to think about around investment accounts. Finally, you will learn the strategies and steps to build, add to, and trim your stock portfolio in a counter-intuitive way that gives you not the guarantee, but a great chance at outperforming the general stock market and achieving the ability to live and retire with financial freedom, whenever that comes, and in whatever form that takes for you.

PART I – FOUNDATION

CHAPTER 1: INVESTING
IS FOR EVERYONE

Purchasing shares of common stock of individual publicly traded companies, or single stock picking, is likely not for everyone. It is certainly not for the faint of heart, and even the bravest of us stock pickers have doubts and fears throughout the process. These feelings can recur weekly or even daily if the stock market movement is generally down for a period of weeks or months, or the sentiment of many investors is in an especially pessimistic mood at the time. If you decide to become a single stock investor, you will have high highs; days, months, or even years you're beating the market, and other days, months, or years you question why you do this at all, as you're getting clobbered much worse than the rest of the market.

You may reach the end of this book and decide single stock picking is not for you, and that is completely okay! The tips that I provide for building a foundation and long-term way to view the markets and organize your financial life, all the steps leading up to single stock picking can be worth it, even if you never buy a single common stock share. Utilizing low-cost index funds, or large groups of stocks wrapped up together, is a great way many people build wealth over time.

Trillions podcast host Eric Valchunez once said that "once investors buy cheap beta; that is, once they get the lowest cost access to simply get market matching returns for a majority of their portfolio via index funds, they often look for some "hot sauce" of higher risk, potentially higher return investments to add to their portfolio." This is in part what this book attempts to help you set up in your own investing life. First you build a foundation, and if you continue on, the single stock portion of your investing portfolio may only ever be the "hot sauce", or a small portion of that portfolio. For others as your comfortability grows, it may become a larger share.

If the foundation of your wealth building journey that we're going to detail is like a cake, then single stock investing can be viewed as the frosting and sprinkles. Not everyone wants frosting and sprinkles on their cake, which is just fine. Frankly, not everyone is cut out emotionally to be a single stock investor. In fact, many people, even some who read this book, should probably avoid it. You can still have a great financial cake without frosting and sprinkles if you choose.

Sadly, many people decide that the whole cake, or investing in the stock market at all, isn't for them. This may have been through personal investing experiences they had that left them scarred with fear of future loss. This could be from a lack of financial education, a belief that they can't afford to invest, or stories they heard from others who fell to financial ruin in the stock market. Or, they may inherently have a hard time with the concept of delayed gratification, and want to live only for the moment, so they don't save or invest. They may have even lost hope of succeeding with money, or fear the economic situation of the future, or many other reasons not listed. This is not a book to shame anyone, but to encourage everyone to begin taking small steps in a positive direction and think about the future with even a bit more hope and practical optimism than you may have now.

The stock market has been the single greatest wealth building tool in history and doesn't have to be an exclusive club. It is surprisingly easier and typically more affordable to begin investing in the stock market than many people realize. You don't have to have millions or even tens of thousands, or even thousands, to begin. But if you don't build a foundation of solid personal finance to get you started, even thinking about investing, let alone actually investing, may feel or be out of reach for some, but hopefully only for a short time.

The takeaways: Even if you never purchase single stocks, learning about the stock market and getting interested in becoming a participant in the stock market is for everyone, don't sit on the sidelines forever. It doesn't take as much money to start investing as you probably think. Single stock investing can start out and remain a very small part of your overall investing journey until you get more comfortable.

Risk

Every decision you make, even the decisions you refuse to make, involve some level of risk. It is a risk to go outside your front door each day. It is an even bigger risk to get into your car and drive anywhere. In fact, your lifetime odds of getting killed in a car crash are about 1 in 93. The more "extreme" the activity, the greater the chance of you getting seriously injured or even killed.

Yet most of us do risk getting in that car, playing recreational sports, spending time outdoors hiking, exercising, visiting friends or family, and doing all these risky activities. We have become comfortable with the level of risk involved. In the back of our minds, we may know these activities have resulted in pain or even death for others, yet we've become accustomed to that risk, and choose to live with the consequences. Choosing never to drive, never to do any recreational activities, never to explore new parts of our world, whether foreign or local, all have their own risks as well.

Choosing never to invest in the stock market certainly has its own risks. Keeping all your money in ultra conservative investments your entire life like cash or cash equivalents carries the risk of that money not growing to keep up with inflation, and not being able to provide you a meaningful source of income in your later years.

Investopedia defines Loss Aversion as "the observation that human beings experience losses asymmetrically more severely than equivalent gains." In other words, losing money hurts us emotionally and psychologically more than gaining money makes us feel good. No wonder so many investors get scared away from investing after a bad loss. That loss is burned in their memory, likely much more than any previous successes they may have had.

When you purchase your first Mutual Fund share, Exchange

Traded Fund (ETF) share, or first share of a company common stock, you may feel scared or nervous. You may feel as if you've just gambled in a casino, and maybe even as if you've made a misstep or mistake if the account doesn't grow immediately. In many people's cases when they are automatically enrolled in a company 401(k) plan when they start a new job, they may not even realize they are already invested in the stock market!

The longer you invest, the more you research and exercise the new muscle of investing, the stronger that muscle gets, and the more relaxed and comfortable with the process you can become. The worst decision you can make is to decide that any form of investing isn't for you.

There are others who do invest in the stock market, but because they never fully understand how it works or are so fearful of losing money, once a major market correction occurs, they get out of the stock market completely and never come back in. This would be akin to getting in a car accident and being afraid to the point of never driving again. I want to teach you the tools to not only understand what investing in the stock market is, but how to set up guardrails against your future self. When you encounter the emotional rollercoaster that investing can be, you'll be able to face it with a cooler head and calmer heart.

To provide a bit more insight into this system, when you invest in the stock market, you are buying shares, either directly or indirectly, in part ownership of a company or group of companies. As a company succeeds or falters in their company revenue (income), profits (income minus costs), growth, and expectations around those metrics for that quarter or year, the stock price may move up or down in reaction. In between quarterly reports, if there is any news that comes out that gives either a positive or negative indication on these earnings metrics, investors and analysts adjust their future expectations of the company or industry by buying or selling shares. This activity of buying or selling causes the price of the stock or stocks to move up or down.

A company can issue more shares, or buy back shares, to increase or decrease the total amount of shares available for purchase by investors. Money only changes hands at the buy and sale of shares. But stocks held can appreciate, meaning go up, or depreciate, meaning go down, and your underlying invested dollars' value follows those price movements. I know this is likely overly simplistic, but I wanted to provide an overview of what the stock market is before moving on.

The takeaways: Risk is unavoidable in life and investing, and determining your own risk tolerance will likely be a moving target throughout your life. The more knowledge you have about what makes investing systems work, the better you'll be able to determine which investing risks to take and be comfortable with, and which risks to avoid. The stock market is a series of buys and sales of part ownership of different companies, and stocks move on these actions.

Investing Vs Saving

Before we move on, I want to split up the terms investing and saving. If you're saving money, this is typically in places like a checking or savings account, or even physical cash on hand. What varies is how easily you can access it, and how much - if any - interest, usually indicated as an annual percentage yield or APY, you are earning on that money. If you have short-term goals such as building and maintaining an emergency fund, or even if you are saving toward a large purchase like a car or a down payment on a home in the next few years, a savings account, an account that can't lose money, is typically a better place to store that money than under your mattress or in the stock market.

There are many online banks that can typically get you higher earning rates than at your local bank or credit union, so I would encourage you to research those options for saving your cash. This savings account would be anything in excess of what you use monthly to pay bills, which would likely be held in a checking account. The reason to not hoard large piles of physical cash is the risk of loss from theft or accidental damage to the money; a bank is typically safer. If you are trying to save for a short-term goal by investing in the stock market hoping to make a quick buck to speed up your savings goal, at the end of that short-term period (even if it's a year or two), it may be a coin flip whether you have made or lost money over that short of a term. A high yield savings account guarantees your additions and has a more predictable return than the stock market in the short term.

We will get more into the nuts and bolts of investing a bit later, I promise, but for now think short-term (less than 3 years): saving. Long-term (more than 3 years): Investing.

The Takeaways: Utilize a checking account for monthly bills and expenses. Move additional cash like an emergency fund or savings goal into a high yield savings account for a better return.

You can often link this account electronically to your checking account for easy transfers. In addition, you're removing the temptation to spend your savings if it's not in the same checking account as your monthly bills. For spending goals of three years or less, save money in a high yield savings account. Four years or more, you can likely do better investing in the stock market.

You Are Where You Are, but That's Not Where You Have to Stay

When it comes to thinking about investing and money, to borrow a phrase from Morgan Housel's *The Psychology of Money*, "you're not crazy." He goes on to say, I'm paraphrasing: "each of you have had a completely unique set of life experiences that have led you to where you are today, and all of those experiences and influences, including even how your generation grew up thinking about money and investing, is unique and real and makes sense to you."

I don't want to take away from your life experiences, and I want to validate the thought that learning to use money well is not an inherent skill we are born with. Most of us weren't taught how to use it well growing up or in school, as our parents likely weren't either. I don't want to shame anyone if they have made any of the mistakes outlined in the next sections, you are where you are. I want to help you create a path forward, knowing that it will likely look different for each of you, to be able to win with money.

Some people may disagree with certain sections of this book, and I welcome that discussion and disagreement. I have learned almost everything I know from taking bits and pieces from a variety of people's opinions and hope you're able to do the same. The last note I want to acknowledge is the likely age and income difference among my readers; I don't want anyone to feel they are too old or too young or don't make enough money to start making smart changes. Although it may be easier for some to align with this path, comparing your life to your peers and wishing you had their life likely won't make you as happy as making positive changes in your own life. The good news is you can begin where you are and with some patience, realistic expectations, and hard work you can begin to shift your financial future in the direction you want to go.

The Takeaways: Everyone's background is unique and likely full of challenges, but you have the chance to decide to improve from this point forward, wherever you are in your life and wealth building journey. Don't lose hope if you're not currently where you want to be. Making small positive financial changes in your life today can compound wonderfully in future years and decades.

CHAPTER 2: SETTING YOUR FINANCIAL FOUNDATION

Please don't skip ahead to the chapters on stock picking. If all this investing and personal finance stuff is new to you, I am so excited to have you read and learn how to set up your financial foundation. If you are very well-read on personal finance, these chapters will be a brief review for you. I have drawn from what I consider the cream of the crop, the best ideas from industry leaders, and you may learn something new. If you disagree with any aspects of these chapters, this is no problem, but don't put down the book, please don't throw the baby out with the bathwater (weird phrase but it fits here).

Things That Could Hold You Back

Consumer Debt. Although some of my readers may roll their eyes when they hear this because of who he is or what they have heard about him, I must acknowledge the large role the teachings of Dave Ramsey had in helping to set the first half of my financial foundation. Although I disagree with a few of his ideas, his overall philosophy of getting out of consumer debt to insulate your financial life, thereby freeing up more of your paycheck towards savings and investing each month, is absolute gold. I also encourage you to have an emergency fund, one of the many principles he teaches.

Life has an annoying habit of trying to wipe out our financial goals just as soon as we're getting in a rhythm and on the path to achieving them. Having anywhere from 3-6 months of your living expenses set in savings can help insulate your life against the unknown and prevent you from cashing out your investments if an emergency does come up and you don't have any emergency cash.

On this subject I also highly recommend the book *Antifragile* by Nassim Teleb, it is a fascinating book about our inability to predict the future despite our attempts to do so, and how it's the unpredictable events that can wipe us out financially. He teaches how to shore up our skills and our finances against many future unknowns, to make ourselves less vulnerable to unexpected changes and more able to adapt with resilience when the unexpected does appear.

Another of Dave Ramsey's principles is paying down your consumer debt as quickly as possible. This constitutes any high-interest debt. This includes car loans, student loans, credit cards that you don't pay off each month, and personal loans or medical debt as the most common categories. Mortgage housing debt is not typically included in consumer debt.

The reason paying down your consumer debt quickly is such

sound advice is that you want the magic of compound interest working for you, not against you. If you're trying to invest heavily in the stock market while still carrying large balances in any of these debt categories, it will lengthen the time you have to pay down that debt as more of your monthly income is tied up in investments instead of paying down debt. Some may argue that you can theoretically earn more each year in investments than your consumer debt rates grow. My counterpoint is that it is hard to outstrip the guaranteed and likely high interest rate that is being charged against you monthly in your consumer debt, with a variable interest rate that you may or may not earn in the stock market in the future, especially over the short-term.

The key is that paying off consumer debt frees up more dollars monthly to be able to invest more for your future. In addition, if you're trying to buy a house along your investing journey, banks look with great scrutiny at how much consumer debt and cash you have relative to your income, as they know these consumer debt monthly obligations may be dollars competing against those earmarked for housing or other living expenses in your monthly budget. If you're interested in more of Dave Ramsey's teaching and philosophy, I encourage you to research his material including his book *The Total Money Makeover*, but that is the extent I will cover it here.

For my own journey, his material and book were very helpful early on in understanding consumer debt better, and paying off my own debts as quickly as I could, to be able to invest more. For me it was a long, 2-year process to pay off my student loans and other bills, but well worth it as it freed up that monthly income to save for a house and invest in the stock market.

The Takeaways: Building an emergency fund in a savings account can help smooth the strain of many unexpected expenses life throws at you. Consumer debt is used for a variety of reasons. It works tirelessly against your wealth building if you hang onto it, usually with compound interest. Holding onto consumer debt makes it harder to have more dollars going into investing accounts each month to build your net worth, so getting rid of the debt as quickly as possible is a great strategy.

A Frugal Mindset is a Driver of Wealth Building

One of the biggest factors in your ability to build wealth over time is your personal behavior, and adopting to at least some extent, a frugal mindset. Frugal does not mean cheap, and it does not even have to mean a low-cost lifestyle, but it does mean living within one's means. If you make $1 million dollars per year, and spend $1.1 million dollars per year, you are not living within your means. It sounds like a ridiculous analogy for most of us, but I have seen many similar cases in real life, though usually with smaller numbers. Personal behavior and living within one's means, or being frugal, is in my opinion one of the largest determining factors if you will be wealthy or not, relative to your lifetime income.

Income, high or low, is not wealth. Income is what you earn, wealth is what you keep. Once you've aggressively paid down your consumer debt, utilizing a monthly budget to be able to "pay yourself first" can be a great start. Paying yourself first means once you receive your monthly paychecks, you transfer an amount of money that you can invest in the stock market each month. You limit yourself to living on the rest of your income for the remainder each month. You'll get used to living on the lower income amount, and not miss the dollars that automatically go to your investment accounts after a few months of doing this. This "pay yourself first" step is more likely to work in building consistent investment habits than saying you'll invest if you have anything left at the end of the month.

We are all human. If we don't do something like earmark and set up automatic deposits away to investment accounts ahead of time, most of us without even thinking about it, will subconsciously increase our spending throughout the month, and there is often nothing left to invest at the end of the month. This is the phrase called lifestyle creep. This also occurs if we're not intentional with any sort of increase to our income throughout the year; our spending subconsciously rises to our income level, and we'll be left scratching our heads when we file our taxes and wonder where all that money went.

The teachings of the late Thomas J Stanley, author of *The Millionaire Next Door* helped drive a controversial theme that many millionaires are wealthy not because they look and act like we think millionaires should, but precisely the opposite; they blend in perfectly with regular society because they have mastered living within their means. This allowed many of them to invest regularly in the stock market throughout their working lives, and build wonderfully large investment portfolios, while their neighbors and friends were clueless to this wealth. They were able to do this because their lifestyle did not creep up with their slowly increasing wealth accumulation. Dr Stanley's daughter, Sarah Stanley Fallaw, wrote a follow-up book which I think might be even better than the original, called *The Next Millionaire Next Door*, researching if the principles and mindset of what Dr Stanley found in the 1990's about successful millionaire behavior, was still true in the 21st century.

I can't recommend this book enough for you to be able to learn even more about the winning mindset of frugality and my favorite phrase from the book, "social indifference". This is the ability to not care what others think about you and your decisions with your life and money. It is a simple concept to think through or to say, yet so hard for many of us to do. If you're going to turn a new page in your life and make some personal financial changes, to be successful, you may need to learn to adopt a level of social indifference in your life.

It is hard to change ingrained behaviors, especially those learned from friends or family. An example of these behaviors is spending everything and more that we earn, so our friends and family think we're doing well financially. Another example is our belief that we deserve to live on more than we make or are entitled to a better life than we can currently afford. If we're able to view our financial lives with a more realistic lens of where we're actually at in the present, we can slowly change the way we think about money and wealth and set some financial goals around how to improve.

These changes won't happen overnight, you will likely have setbacks along the way. Making changes will set the foundation for you to feel more grounded, become a more successful investor, and eventually, the ability to have much more wealth than you have today. This book, *The Next Millionaire Next Door*, cemented many ideas I already had about wealthy people and how they got there. It also gave me a good guide for patterns of behavior to live in my own life. It has helped me always pay myself first by investing regularly, and to do my best to not care what others think about me, especially when it comes to purchases of material things.

The Takeaways: Income is not wealth. Income is what you earn, wealth is what you keep. Whatever your current income, striving to keep more of it and turn it into wealth through improved spending, saving, and investing habits can slowly change the course of your financial future for the better.

F.I.R.E.

I am not one who gets giddy thinking about dying with a big pile of money to donate to charity or give to my heirs. While these are honorable goals, my goals for investing were initially more in line with the FIRE (Financially Independent Retire Early) community. This community explores different ways to get to the point where you can choose whether to work, and to what extent, instead of having no choice but to work your whole life to pay bills. They advocate extremely high savings rates (percent of your income you put toward investments) as part of getting to that financial independence early. I have great respect for members of this community, their discipline is impressive. Like these other two examples I listed with Ramsey and Stanley above, I don't ascribe to every single part of the FIRE community but like to take what I view is the best from each.

From the FIRE community, my takeaway is that you are decades or less away from financial freedom, but a lot of it comes down to your savings rate and what you're willing to sacrifice to get there. I don't think I will ever want to get to an amazingly high 50% savings rate as some in the community ascribe, but I love the mentality around seeing how far you can stretch yourself, if this is the direction you choose to go. I don't think I will retire before age 60 either, mostly because I enjoy working quite a bit, but you never know what life can throw at you.

One of the biggest benefits of having money is it gives you options. Even if you increase your savings rate as is taught by Ramsey and the Millionaire Next Door or even further up to the FIRE community recommendations and never retire early, there are options as a frugal saver you unlock, that you may not otherwise, if you're forced to continue living paycheck to paycheck indefinitely. Having options gives you hope, feeling like you have no choices in life feels hopeless. Examples of options unlocked with financial independence could include changing jobs to a lower paying job that gives you more flexibility or is more aligned with your values, or in a different area you want to live. It could also mean having the ability to take significant time off due to health or family reasons if needed. It could even mean going down to part-time work in your last decade or decades before full retirement, to pursue hobbies or other interests.

The last thing on setting a personal finance foundation is this; if you don't have any money, you are more likely to find yourself in situations where you're forced to make tough decisions out of desperation, this is sadly the reality for so many people. Setting a financial foundation before investing can prevent (of course not all) but many of those hardships from forcing you to sell your investments to cover life's emergencies. When you're able to build some short-term savings, get out of consumer debt, and increase your savings rate, you give yourself the best chance to build wealth, and the options to mold your future life differently. You have hope when it comes to money, maybe for the first time in your life. That is the biggest reason to start this tough yet rewarding path.

The Takeaways: Whatever your goals or eventual savings rate, pushing yourself to improve your financial foundation gives you options and hope about your future that you may not have otherwise. Greater financial discipline now, wherever you're at, can provide greater life flexibility for you in the future.

Long-term View of the Market and Savings Rate

Sitting on the sidelines cannot be an option for you if you want to build wealth. Due to the power of compound interest over time, (your money's ability to make you more money), keeping all your money in cash, checking accounts, even money market accounts or CD's, does not hold a candle to the long-term returns of the stock market.

It can make sense at different times in your life to hold some of your funds in these savings accounts, however the key term is they are savings accounts, not investment accounts. Remember that savings are for relatively short-term needs, anticipated or unanticipated. Getting invested in the stock market through equities, or shares of companies, for long durations is how investors can build wealth over time, not through relatively low yields in cash or CD's. I am not a huge fan of bonds as we'll discuss later, but many investors use those as a generally lower risk and lower returning option alongside stocks.

Of course, there are years where the stock market does go down, and in some cases quite dramatically, even for extended periods of time. This is when some media headlines love to point out that if you had been invested in cash during that year instead of the stock market, you would have outperformed everyone in the stock market. But this myopic, or near-sighted view, has its drawbacks. If you were so smart as to time the stock market and get out at the right peak before a crash - congratulations. Now how will you know when the right time is to get back in?

History has shown that many stock market bottoms have occurred long before people realize, and by the time the markets have gone back up, those on the sidelines may be thinking they missed the wave and will be watching for a future drawdown again to re-enter, missing out on some of the biggest returns of the market. This is a stressful way to invest for almost anyone and would likely be filled with frustration. Instead, set up your financial life in a way where you don't need your investment dollars to live on in the short or medium term. As gut-wrenching as it can sometimes be to watch the swings in the market, buy great companies (or groups of companies if you choose to go that route), and continue to buy each month. Leave your stocks alone for extended periods. This has been shown to be the superior strategy over the decades when comparing long-term stock market returns to cash, and it's not even close.

A book that is so full of wisdom on this point is *Stocks for the Long Run* by Jeremy Siegel. I will admit it's not an easy read for me, it has stretches that are tough to get through, but is full of ironclad data and historical figures that exemplify the way that investing in stocks has proven the most enduring asset class to own over the decades and even centuries.

Before we get on to single stock picking, I want to acknowledge if more investors did just seek and achieve average stock market returns over the decades, this is a good strategy. I believe everyone should be invested in the market, and a good chunk of that wealth can be invested successfully in boring stock indexes, through large funds (mutual funds or ETFs, we can get into that later) that hold nearly all the stocks in the stock market. This is not only a good idea, but for most of my readers, likely a necessary starting point.

I have read many great books about the long-term view of the stock market, and many of the authors are skeptical if not downright mocking of single stock investing, assigning it to the same category as playing the slots at a casino or horse-race gambling, recommending only index funds or mutual funds to the common investor.

It is hard to argue with hundreds of years of historical data showing that getting average market returns, not more or less, can be a powerful wealth-building tool for many investors. As I mentioned at the outset of the book, if you never take the final step toward single stock investing yet follow these other steps in setting up a firm financial foundation and invest with the idea of getting the average market returns, this could be a great strategy for you. I haven't stopped there though with this book, because I believe there are many benefits to being a "small" retail investor buying single company stocks. This can give you not a guarantee but a chance to outperform the market averages and build outsized wealth.

The Takeaways: Investing to get average market returns in the stock market is a great starting goal, many investors do much worse by trading in and out of the market too frequently. Market timing is very challenging. It is better to shore up your financial life so you can consistently buy stocks each month and not have to worry about short-term returns. Stocks have proved to be the highest returning asset class, but the most volatile, with single stock investing being even more volatile than index investing. Single stock investing carries more risk but has greater opportunities of outperformance than index investing.

CHAPTER 3: LET'S GET INVESTING

401(k)

Once you have shored up your personal finance foundation as outlined previously, you're ready to invest. I hope to have readers of all ages read this book, so later in the book, I want to go through how your Stock Planting ™ system will apply in different decades of your life. I don't want to mention age groups at this point, but it is important, and will be addressed later.

One of the largest wealth-building tools many Americans have access to is their company 401(k) or 403(b) plans. If your company does not offer a 401(k) or 403(b), do not be dismayed, you can nearly replicate a 401(k) with a bit of work, through Individual Retirement Arrangements, or IRA's. I will get to IRA's right after 401(k) plans. A 403(b) plan is typically for teachers and government workers, but functions very similarly to 401(k) plans, so for simplicity I will refer to 401(k) alone and not both.

A 401(k) is a relatively boring investment instrument. Remember that all retirement accounts are a wrapper (like on your favorite candy bar). It is a tax designation so the IRS knows how to treat the account, it does not indicate what the underlying account is invested in. Its name is taken from the tax code from which the plan was presented, nothing flashier than that. The 401(k) plan permits your employer to withhold a percentage of your paycheck and invest it, per your investment elections, or choices, typically in line with your pay period. If you are getting paid bi-weekly, you would contribute every other week, etc. A 401(k) plan is required by what are called safe harbor laws to have a mix of investments you can choose from that are diversified, or different from one another. This typically means some different types of stock funds, bond funds, real estate funds, possibly commodity funds, and cash equivalent funds, maybe others.

If you have access to a 401(k) plan and have never invested in it, once you shore up your financial foundation, it could be a good idea to start there, especially if your employer offers a match. If your employer offers a match, that means they will contribute a dollar amount or percentage with company money to your 401(k)-retirement account in line with your contributions. This is one of the easiest ways to increase, in some cases double the amount of money you are investing per paycheck, and taking advantage of a company's match has been a large part of many investors' wealth building journey. There may be a vesting period, a time that the employer will hold but not give you their match, until you work so many years at that job, to incentivize you to stay longer. Each plan is set up a bit differently. You can ask your HR personnel any plan specifics you need to feel comfortable with the account, and they may have access to a financial advisor you could ask even more questions to, if needed.

The Takeaways: A 401(k) plan is a workplace retirement account that allows your employer to contribute from your paycheck directly into a retirement account in your name. They may add additional company funds, called a match. A 401(k) plan can be a great place to start for beginners new to investing, especially if there is an attractive company match.

What Do You Invest in Within your 401(k)?

I want to be careful not to give specific fund advice in this book, as I want to help you peel away the mysticism around investing and become more confident in your own investing abilities. As you start to understand the stock market, investment accounts, and develop the right expectations about investing, your fear and anxiety can subside, and you can choose your own funds and later your own stocks to invest in.

Although I won't tell you what specific funds to invest in, I can give very general types of funds I like and don't like, and why, and you can do your own research and make your own decisions from there.

Generally, most funds, or large groups of stocks and bonds lumped together, available in 401(k) plans are called Mutual Funds. These funds are made up of a large group of investors' money pooled together and are referred to as open-ended. This means they can accept nearly any dollar amount to invest. This is how the same mutual funds can be available for large investment amounts, or very small amounts, making them inclusionary for most investors. Due to this ability to accept any dollar amount, mutual funds are a good fit for 401(k) plans and HSA (Health Savings Accounts) but I think there are better alternatives than mutual funds once we're outside of 401(k) plans.

For this section on your 401(k), if you're interested in further reading, although it is quite a long book, I recommend Tony Robbins *Money: Master the Game*. Yes, it's the self-help guru guy, but he really did his homework and talked to some incredibly successful investors to put this book together. If you are intimidated by a 21-hour audiobook about finance, he wrote another book, *Unshakeable*, which is very similar, yet condensed down to 7 hours.

As part of the book, he does a great deep dive into different types of Mutual Funds and focuses a lot on the impact of various fund and plan fees, and how high fees in your 401(k) plan can drag on your ultimate wealth building ability. Fees get paid out of your account in a 401(k) plan whether you make money each year or not, so not being obsessed, but paying attention to your fund fees is an important aspect to your 401(k)-investing success.

Most people don't realize that within their 401(k) plan, the selection of funds can have massively different ranges of fees, anywhere from 0.4% to over 2%. While these numbers seem relatively small, if you take say a 1% difference over the course of your working life and hopefully the tens of thousands you'll contribute and let grow over decades, the higher fees can make a large difference in your wealth accumulated within the plan at the end of your working life, due to less dollars taking advantage of compound interest over the decades.

I encourage you after reading this section to look up some of the funds you have chosen within your 401(k) plan if you've already been investing in a plan, and look up the expense ratio, or management fee, on the funds by a quick internet search of the fund Ticker, which is the sequence of letters that uniquely describe that fund. While this expense ratio doesn't cover all fees in your mutual funds, as there are additional administrative fees from the 3rd party company investing for you, it can start to give you an idea of what type of preliminary fees there are on the funds you're invested in.

I like Mutual Funds with the broadest stock market exposure, as these generally have lower fees, but not always. Broad equity exposure means they carry a very high number of stocks within the fund across many industries, and usually don't sell stocks often within the fund, which helps keep costs low. I don't have an issue with selecting specific funds based on industries, I do a little of that myself. But you may find that the more focused and specific the strategy, the higher the management fee (expense ratio), as those funds may require more active management (buying and selling) by the fund manager - the person or group actively investing within the mutual fund. This can certainly pay off with some funds, not as much for others. Diversifying, or having a variety of investments within your 401(k) plan should be to your comfort level.

Funds that are tough for me to fully get behind are Bond Funds, and Target Date Funds. Both are very popular options within 401(k) plans, and if you choose to invest in them, it will not be the end of the world, but it is worth pausing to think through why you may or may not choose them.

The Takeaways: Investing in your 401(k) plan is not very exciting but can be a great way to get extra dollars working for your retirement especially with a company match, through consistent paycheck deductions. A good place to start is by searching out the funds available to you with the broadest market exposure that are made up of many stocks and have low expense ratios. Be mindful of specific strategy fund expense ratios and overall 401(k) administrative plan fees, which may have a small to large impact on your account's ability to grow.

Bonds

To understand bond funds which are popular options within 401(k) plans, it helps to understand bonds a bit better. Unlike common stock, which is part ownership in a company, a bond is a contract, or debt obligation, typically with a fixed payout and fixed time horizon for that payout. Interest payments may be made twice per year, once per year, or not at all until the end of the contract, depending on how the specific contract is set up.

With a bond, if you hold it until maturity, or the length of the contract, you can get your money back plus interest. These are generally viewed as safer and more conservative investment options than stocks, so many recommend having a mix of stocks and bonds. However, with many bond funds, which are bunches of bonds grouped together, there is no fixed maturity. The fund manager must continuously buy and sell bonds of varying price and maturity, so you don't often get as much relative safety of a single bond, as there may not be a fixed redemption date. In addition, bonds and especially bond funds are susceptible to interest-rate risk, meaning that as interest rates rise, a bond's price can go down.

In addition, the longer the maturity period of the bond, called its duration, the more volatile the price will react in the short term to interest rate movements. My point here is that while bonds have long been viewed as the less risky alternative to stocks, which can be true in some scenarios especially shorter term, they are not without risk, especially in bond funds. I believe specific bonds, especially municipal bonds, could have their place in high-net worth investors' portfolios, or a strategy of laddering specific individual bonds could be viable for others. For most investors with long time horizons, especially younger investors, in my opinion they are not as great an option as stocks.

In fact, it is my opinion that generally young investors are likely not taking enough risk, given their hopefully very long time-horizon for investing. Over the short term, such as over various one- or two-year periods, bonds can outperform stocks and are thus championed as playing a part in investors' portfolios. Although viewed as less risky than stocks, bonds can go down in tandem with stocks during certain market cycles, they do not always perform the opposite to stocks, as some believe.

Jeremy Siegel said in his book *Stocks for the Long Run*, "Out of all asset classes, only stocks have proven themselves powerful enough to overcome inflation over the long run."

In the foreword to his book, Jeremy distinguished the difference in expectations an investor should have between stocks and bonds. He said: "There is overwhelming reason to believe that stocks will remain the best investment for those seeking steady, long-term gains. The risk premium earned by equities over the long run must remain intact if the system is to survive. Bonds cannot, and should not, outperform equities over the long run. Bonds are contracts, enforceable in court by law. Equities promise nothing. Stocks are risky investments involving a high degree of faith in the future. Thus, equities are not inherently "better" than bonds, but we demand a higher return from equities to compensate for their risk."

Some of you may still find use for bonds in your 401(k) plans or elsewhere, and I'm not upset about that, please take the good points that you can from this book and go on to make your own investing system even better than mine!

The Takeaways: Bonds, especially bond funds, are likely not as riskless as you may think, especially considering the opportunity cost of investing in stocks if you're on the younger end of the age spectrum. If you want some of your funds at less risk than stocks, many 401(k) plans have a cash or money market option you could substitute for part or all your bond allocation, with the rest in stocks. If you choose to invest in bonds, no problem, but try to understand the funds you're getting into.

Target Date Funds

These funds have been incredibly popular in recent years in 401(k) plans, as they have been marketed as a "set it and forget it" approach for those who don't want to think about their portfolio. I acknowledge that there are many people that truly don't care to even look at their 401(k) plan for several years or even decades, so it may make sense for them to use one of these target date funds. In fact, many of the funds have specific years you are targeting for retirement, often listed in the name of the fund itself. The strategy is to be riskier in the earlier part of your working career, and as you get closer to that target date, your account funds will "automatically" be taken out of a high percentage of risky equity investments, and into a higher percentage of bonds, bond funds, and cash. While I like the overall principle of de-risking as you approach retirement, the typically high fees associated with these target date funds — usually over 1-2% — make this option tough for me to get behind. I want to acknowledge that there has been an improvement in recent years in expense ratios for target date funds, they have started to come down, so I'm not quite as opposed to them as I once was.

Tony Robbins goes through these target date funds in depth in his book that I mentioned earlier, which is what first put them on my radar. What we learned in the previous section about bond funds makes target date funds even less appealing to me. This is because your portfolio makes the "less risky" higher shift to bonds as you get older, but it may not be as conservative as you think. While there are different investor types and market cycles where bonds could make sense, please keep your eyes wide open to the difference between stocks and bonds for the long-term, and what underlying assets you are invested in within your company retirement plan, and why. If you want to meet with a financial advisor to go over the specific funds and where they may make sense in your portfolio, that can be a great idea. The likely audience of this book is primarily for DIY, the

Do-It-Yourself crowd, so such a meeting may not be necessary for everyone. Continue to read and study, and with enough time, these items that can seem overwhelming or complex at first can become manageable and even mundane over time.

The Takeaways: target date funds can be a good fit for the absent investor who doesn't want to think about investing or retirement for decades, but I think you can find better options within your 401(k) plan if you dig around and are interested in doing so. As with all mutual funds within your 401(k) plan, be mindful of fees if you do select a Target Date Fund.

401(k) Advantages

There are many benefits to a 401(k) or 403(b) retirement plan if your company offers one. It is relatively easy to get set up through your workplace and is managed by a third-party administrator. All you must do is pick the funds, pick the percent of your paycheck that will go into them, and that is about it. Mutual funds are the most common investment within a 401(k) plan, due to their open-ended ability to take any dollar amount and get it invested in the fund. The biggest advantage of a 401(k) is if your company provides a match, you get some free money from your company deposited along with your money each month. The yearly contribution amount on 401(k) plans is also much higher than IRA's, (Traditional or Roth) as well. The 401(k) plan is a great tool for those who want to build a retirement nest egg, but don't want to think about it very much along the way.

401(k) Disadvantages

There can be a limited menu of investment options within your 401(k) plan, you're not able to invest in whatever security (investment) you'd like as you can with either type of IRA or an after tax investment account. The industry is changing, but often you are limited only to mutual funds and excluded from owning ETFs or single stocks in your 401(k) plan. In addition to the expense ratios and management fees of the mutual funds themselves, your account will have administrative management fees with at least a portion of those fees coming directly from your account. It can be hard to decipher your plan fees, most plans don't exactly make it easy to determine how much you're systematically getting charged, whether your account performs well each year or not.

Additionally, in some plans, administrators will prorate and draw a larger percent of the administration fees from the larger accounts in your company plan. You could be penalized if you're a top saver among your peers, or if relatively very few of your peers are contributing, and you'll likely never know. I love the idea of contributing to get some or all of the company match with 401(k) plans to get that instant free money from your employer, but nothing above the match. As you will see throughout the remainder of the book, I believe there are lower-fee and higher alpha (chance at market outperformance) ways of investing on your own above the match. Your goal with the 401(k) plan should not be outperforming the market but selecting funds to limit fees just to match the market, making a strong yet dull backbone to your portfolio, permitting you to take more risk in your other investing accounts.

401(k) Wrap-up

Before we move on from this point, if your company does not offer a 401(k) or 403(b) plan, you can still build the backbone of your portfolio and have a similar experience to the 401(k) plan participants. You can do this by opening a Traditional or Roth IRA and regularly buying the same types of index funds through large market, low-cost mutual funds or Exchange Traded Funds (ETFs). Although you may not be getting a match, you can still have that large portion of your portfolio attempting to simply match the overall market returns, providing a base layer for your investing. As a silver lining to alleviate the sting of not getting a company match in your IRA, a positive way you could think about it if you're in this situation is that you're not being charged a 401(k)-administration fee, in addition to the fund fee, by going this route.

Okay. Now if you're following along in the book, hypothetically you have built some emergency savings, learned to live on less than you make, and have started investing, possibly partly or completely up to the company match in your company 401(k) plan. You have taken some time to go through your available 401(k) plan funds, and have made your own personalized selection, and utilized the help of a financial advisor if needed. You generally know what makes a good mutual fund and are ready for more. The question comes up, as you get raises in the future and are running this system, why invest in single stocks at all? Why not incrementally build up to where you can max out your 401(k) contributions and keep it as simple as that?

As I mentioned in the outset of the book, if this is as far as you want to go, I have met many retirees who have followed some version of the simple system outlined thus far throughout their lives, and were able to build wealth over the decades just fine. There is nothing wrong with this! But I don't think you purchased this book to stop here with the 401(k), as I wasn't fully satisfied there wasn't more out there when I reached this level, either.

CHAPTER 4: TAX QUALIFICATION OF INVESTMENT ACCOUNTS

Before we get into the nuts and bolts of the Stock Planting ™ system, it is important to choose which type of account or accounts you will use to implement the system. It can work in a variety of account types, with each having their advantages and disadvantages.

I want to go through some pros and cons of the tax qualifications of the various types of investing accounts. This is important because there are different tax consequences both along the way growing your account and again when you ultimately tap into the respective accounts for income (sell positions or distribute from the account). I must reiterate what I said from the start, this book is not specific investment advice, and that applies here to the types of investment accounts. I will state my opinion of what I view as some of the pros and cons of each of the different types of investment accounts and why they may or may not be a good idea in various situations, but please do your own research and consult a tax or estate expert if needed for additional clarification.

To understand the tax qualification system, understanding the terms Qualified and non-Qualified can be very helpful to start. A Qualified account is one that is given special tax treatment by the IRS. To get and maintain that tax treatment, you must comply with a set of rules around the account. Qualified accounts include Traditional 401(k)'s, Roth-eligible 401(k)'s, 403(b)'s, 457 plans, Traditional IRAs, and Roth IRAs. There are more, but these are the most common types. Qualified accounts are rightly often referred to as retirement accounts because you typically cannot access them until later in your life, when you are nearing retirement.

Although there are more rules than just age, we'll try to keep it simple for this book. You typically cannot take withdrawals from a Qualified account until you are 59.5 years old without paying a penalty. In return, the IRS lets you have tax-deferred (delayed) or tax-free growth on your account, depending on the type. A Non-qualified account is a non-retirement account, and there are other rules associated with that type of account that we'll get into a bit later.

The takeaways: Qualified accounts are retirement accounts, meant for later in life. The IRS gives special tax treatment to different accounts, like a defining blanket around the underlying investment. Non-Qualified accounts have more flexibility and can be used for purposes other than retirement but come along with their own rules too. There is not as much special treatment from the IRS for Non-Qualified accounts, but less restrictions too.

Traditional Retirement Accounts

Traditional means pre-tax. For most except the highest of earners, you get to deduct the contributions from your taxable income on an annual basis in most Traditional retirement plans, including Traditional 401(k) and Traditional IRA's (Individual Retirement Arrangements). This lowers your taxable income for the year, which is a big advantage. While you get a tax deduction today for those dollars contributed, the invested dollars also get to grow tax-deferred, which means you don't pay taxes on the contributions, growth, or dividends in your investment account until you withdraw funds from the account. In addition, you can buy or sell funds within these types of accounts and incur no taxes or penalties as long as the funds all stay behind the tax wall, as pre-tax funds. A downside to the Traditional 401(k) or Traditional IRA is that all contributions and growth are fully taxable as ordinary income upon withdrawal. This can be a significant tax bill in retirement, since the majority of people's retirement account is made up of the growth and not contribution by the time they withdraw the money, but it all gets the same fully taxable treatment.

If you move funds out of a pretax or Traditional account and into a checking or savings account, this passing of the tax wall triggers a taxable event, and the funds move from Qualified to Non-Qualified. If you're under age 59.5 you get a penalty amount you owe in addition to the taxes incurred, except for special circumstances. If you change jobs, you can roll your 401(k) to your new 401(k) plan at your new job or to a Traditional IRA for more control over what is invested. I like the second option better, rolling into an IRA, unless you'd rather stay hands-off with the management of the account. Not likely if you're reading this book!

If you had only pretax funds in your 401(k), all would have to go to a Traditional IRA to avoid taxes or penalties. If you have a mix of Traditional 401(k) and Roth 401(k) funds, the corresponding amounts in your 401(k) would go to each type of IRA, you will need to open 2 separate accounts, one Traditional IRA, and the other Roth IRA.

The Takeaways: Traditional (pretax) retirement accounts feel better as you contribute, as you get tax deductions on your income taxes in the year you contribute and tax-deferred growth in the accounts. They can be more of a tax pain upon eventual withdrawal in retirement.

IRA Advantages

Why invest in an IRA instead of only in your 401(k) plan? As mentioned previously, a main advantage of the IRA route instead of or in addition to the 401(k) plan is flexibility. You can open a Traditional or Roth IRA through a number of online brokerages and much more easily implement your Stock Planting ™ system in one of these accounts than your 401(k). You don't have to move or adjust your brokerage accounts around changing jobs like you do with the 401(k). Most brokerage accounts are low cost, and the fees in an IRA are typically lower than investing through a 401(k). You can also invest in whatever you'd like: mutual funds, ETFs, single stocks, REITs (more on those later) and other securities.

There is another advantage for Traditional and Roth IRAs over 401(k) plans. If you are married and only one of you works, you can open an IRA for yourself, and open a spousal IRA for your spouse if you have dollar-for-dollar income from wages or employment to match your contributions. You cannot contribute to an IRA of either type if you don't have earned income in a given year. There is no spousal 401(k) option, those plans must be tied to the employee only.

IRA Disadvantages

There is a limit to your annual contribution in either Traditional or Roth IRA that is much lower than the limit for 401(k) plans. You cannot maximum fund both a Traditional and Roth IRA, it is up to the maximum limit for both types. You could do some of your investing dollars into each type of IRA each year or all contributions into just one or the other, it is one total IRA limit annually. I want to repeat the biggest disadvantage of Traditional IRA which applies to Traditional 401(k) as well. While you do get tax-deferred status on the account and a tax deduction on funds going in, eventually you will likely want or need to take withdrawals in retirement. All withdrawals are fully taxable at the higher tax level of ordinary income, not the lower capital gains rate, whether that be account contribution or growth. As an example, if you contributed $150,000 to a Traditional IRA over the course of your working lifetime and that account grew to a total of $1,000,000 by the time you retire, you would owe taxes on all $1,000,000. Even though you got tax deductions each year for the $150,000 contributions along the way, that $1,000,000 will all be fully taxable as you withdraw it in retirement.

The Takeaways: Taxes matter, as much as we'd all like to avoid thinking about them. While retirement may be a long way away for many of you, thinking through what types of accounts you'd like to have when you do retire, can be a great exercise now.

Roth Retirement Accounts

The second type of Qualified account, the Roth, is my personal favorite. While you don't get any tax deduction for contributing to either a Roth 401(k) or Roth IRA, since you'll be funding it with after-tax dollars, if you wait until age 59.5 and the account has been open for at least 5 years, all withdrawals are tax-free! This includes contributions and growth, which can be a significant difference if you're investing over decades. Like the Traditional IRA, you can buy and sell investments within your Roth IRA without incurring taxes, and pay no capital gains or taxes on dividends. Unlike the Traditional IRA, as long as you keep the funds on the right side of the tax wall and follow the age limitation and 5-year rule, all account growth, which will similarly make up a larger portion of your account than contributions by the time you retire, can be yours completely tax-free.

Roth IRA Advantages

A Roth IRA, similar to a Roth-eligible 401(k), is funded with after-tax dollars. It grows tax-free, and after age 59.5 distributions to your checking account for spending will be tax-free, withdrawals and growth included. You can buy or sell whatever investments you'd like within this account, without tax implications. These rules make the Roth IRA my personal favorite of the types mentioned. Returning to that example above, if you contributed $150,000 to a Roth IRA over the course of your working lifetime and it grew the same as above, although you didn't get a tax deduction each year on the contributions, you get to enjoy all $1,000,000 tax-free as you withdraw it in retirement.

Roth IRA Disadvantages

High income earners are eventually phased out of being able to contribute to a Roth IRA by their level of income, so if you're close to the limit in a given year, watch carefully to make sure you don't have to deal with going over the income limit and the hassle of retracting excess contributions. Another disadvantage commonly brought up is that you don't get to deduct the contributions for taxes in that current year, increasing your taxable income each year by going with Roth instead of Traditional, no matter how the account performs.

The Takeaways: Pay more taxes now or pay more later, that is the choice with Traditional vs Roth accounts, you can't escape taxes with investing in retirement accounts. I can't say which would be better for you, you could have some of each type or just one, but I love the flexibility in investment options that both IRA's provide.

Non-Qualified Accounts

Non-Qualified accounts are not retirement accounts. They are easiest to think about when you relate them to checking or savings accounts, but they are accounts in which you can buy and sell investments, instead of just sitting in cash, as is typical with checking or savings. They are also called post-tax brokerage accounts and can be owned by one person or as a joint account by multiple people.

Non-Qualified Account Advantages

You have incredible flexibility with contributing to and withdrawing from these accounts. You can easily link them to your checking account via ACH connection. This stands for Automatic Clearing House, it means a bank to bank connection. With this connection, you can transfer money electronically within a few days back and forth from your checking account. There are no income limits or age restrictions to worry about like with retirement accounts. You have the similar flexibility of both types of IRAs to buy and sell whatever type of security or investment you want, unlike the 401(k) plans.

You will pay taxes when you sell positions that have appreciated (grown) above what you paid for them, that is called a capital gain. If you sell positions at a loss, you can deduct a portion of that loss from your taxes. You are not taxed for capital gains until you sell a position, and the tax rate changes whether you sell within one year of purchase or hold the position at least one year or more. If you hold onto a position for at least one year, it is generally a more favorable tax rate than the ordinary income tax rate when you do sell. You can sell and withdraw the funds as you need throughout your life from a Non-Qualified account, not only in retirement.

The flexibility and ability to access the funds before retirement age make non-Qualified accounts my second-favorite type of investment account. You could think of this type of investment account as a long-term extension of your emergency fund, or a very long-term saving account, but please keep the core of your emergency fund in cash, as your investment account could drop in value unexpectedly, right when you have an emergency. Life can be weird that way. You don't want to interrupt compound interest and tap into this account unless you absolutely have to, but it would still be more advantageous in most circumstances to do so, than to tap into your retirement accounts early, and incur penalties and miss out on tax-deferred or tax-free growth intended for later in your life.

Non-Qualified Account Disadvantages

You are taxed on dividend income each year when you receive dividends in a non-qualified account. This is true whether you move the dividends to your checking account and spend them, reinvest the dividends into more stocks within your investment account, or even if the dividends just accumulate in your account. We will cover dividends in more detail later in the book. You are taxed for dividends typically at the preferred lower capital gains rate, but it is still realized income each year that needs to be reported and taxed.

In addition, when you do eventually sell positions in a non-qualified account, you may have a low cost-basis (low starting price) if you have held the positions for long periods of time and they have gone up in value. You may have a very large tax bill waiting for you that year, as everything in between your purchased price and sale price is taxable gain. If you find yourself in that great situation, meeting with a tax expert before you sell can be very beneficial.

The Takeaways: non-Qualified accounts offer great flexibility. The funds held within can be withdrawn at any time throughout your life and can be used as a great savings tool for non-retirement long-term goals. Holding investments for longer time periods gives you some tax efficiency, but ultimately the flexibility you get from investing in a non-qualified account is the tradeoff of less overall tax efficiency that you get from Qualified investment accounts. When you do sell positions in a Non-Qualified account, there will always be some taxable event.

When To Use Each Type of Account

Now that we have gone over the various types of investment accounts, you can apply them to the full Stock Planting ™ system you'll soon learn. After you've established your high-yield savings account for emergency funds and short-term purchases and have invested either partly or fully up to the match if you have a company 401(k), you could next look at either a Traditional or Roth IRA at a brokerage company where you have lots of flexibility and control for your Stock Planting ™. Whether you can or want to max out the contributions of your IRA or IRA's is completely dependent on your situation. Lastly, a non-qualified investment account at a brokerage company is a great place to finish.

There are many who advocate maxing out and focus only on Qualified retirement accounts such as 401(k) plans and IRAs, but I like the idea of having a non-Qualified bridge account, or a freedom fund as others call it. What if you want to retire before age 59.5? What if you need some money along the way for any number of things, including large financial emergencies that you can't predict? Adding at least a portion of your investing dollars each month in a taxable non-Qualified account can make a lot of sense. It can give you flexibility and options that you otherwise may not have. If you don't want to invest in a non-qualified account, increasing your emergency cash to a higher level may be an alternative step some may want to take; it varies from person to person. Do everything you can to avoid tapping into your Qualified retirement accounts early and incurring unnecessary penalties and taxes and robbing yourself of compound interest in those accounts.

As you go through different seasons of life, personal incomes and the percentage of your income you add to varying investment accounts may change as well. But as time goes on, you'll also get increasingly comfortable with your own setup, and likely continue to dial in what the best strategies are for your current situation. I want to help you feel comfortable investing for the long term, and I'm here to guide you!

The Takeaways: Everyone's preferred mix of account types will be different, but understanding the pros and cons of each is so important, and why I spent so much time going over them. I wanted to jump straight to Stock Planting ™ right away in this book but realized without this framework of investment account options I've laid out, it could be easy to make mistakes or become overwhelmed.

CHAPTER 5: FUND TYPES IN VARIOUS ACCOUNTS

Now that you've learned more about the various types of investing accounts and where each might be applicable in your Stock Planting ™ system, I want to briefly review some types of funds you may encounter within the different accounts, and under what circumstances it might make sense to use each one.

Mutual Fund Pros

The biggest advantage of mutual funds is that they are open-ended; you can add any dollar amount per month, great or small, and partial shares will be invested for you, in a large pool with "mutual" other investors' dollars. These funds are commonly used in qualified account plans such as a 401(k), 403(b), or HSA, (Health Savings Accounts). There is an incredible variety of mutual funds, with different goals for various sectors of the market. The price changes only once per day at the end of the trading day and is based on the NAV or Net Asset Value, that is inflows and outflows of money into or out of the fund, divided by the total number of shares. This can be an advantage for new or nervous investors, the price doesn't fluctuate as much as with stocks or ETFs.

Mutual Fund Cons

These funds have an expense ratio, where the fund manager gets a fee for investing your dollars in their fund no matter how it performs. There are varying setups with mutual fund fees, even including some advertising fees to attract other investors. Each fee setup may make sense in different situations and holding periods for investors with different goals. Mutual funds are often least attractive in taxable or non-qualified accounts, as you may have capital gains each year even if you personally don't sell shares. If the fund manager must sell some shares to cover other shareholders' redemptions (withdrawals) from the fund, you may be taxed. This is not very tax-efficient for non-qualified accounts, which is one of the reasons ETFs were created.

The Takeaways: Mutual Funds are great in qualified retirement plans due to their ability to accept any amount of your monthly paycheck contributions into the fund. They are less great in non-qualified accounts, and do have a management fee called an expense ratio.

Exchange Traded Funds (ETF) Pros

ETFs are groups of stocks or other securities chosen by fund managers, like mutual funds. The difference is ETFs are closed-ended, meaning the price changes throughout the trading day as shares are bought and sold, like single stocks. This gives a real-time price change to investors more concerned with the short-term gains or losses on a fund. ETFs are more tax-efficient than mutual funds in taxable non-qualified accounts, as you don't get taxed each year for capital gains if you don't sell shares, and you are only taxed when you sell a position. You are taxed for dividends each year if your ETFs are within that post-tax account, like stocks and mutual funds.

Another advantage is that there are some ETFs that broadly cover large portions of the market for very low expense ratios and rarely turn over positions (buy and sell). These ETFs can help you closely match the overall market performance in this way. There are many other ETFs that are targeted by sector and preferred by thematic investors, or someone trying to catch a trend in an industry sector. If you want access to a particular sector or even subsector of the market, you could buy an ETF that covers a specific strategy or small portion of that industry instead of having to own many single separate shares of that sector in single stocks.

For those who want to start out with ETFs then move to single stocks when they feel comfortable, ETFs can be a great starter option, they fit well within the Stock Planting ™ system due to their closed-end nature. You would likely hold ETFs in your Traditional and Roth IRA as well as taxable non-Qualified accounts. You can track the daily and total percent accumulation (growth) the position has earned for you, very similar to a single company stock. My first couple of investments in my own investment account years ago were ETFs, and after a month of watching how they worked I felt comfortable moving on to single stocks.

ETF Cons

Unlike a mutual fund, if you're doing the whole shares approach and not the fractional share approach, you cannot purchase a small portion of an ETF monthly unless you have the whole dollar amount of the share price each time. You would have to wait and save up and buy each ETF share individually unless you're on a platform that permits the purchase of fractional shares. While many ETFs are inexpensive, some can be several hundreds of dollars per share. Unlike single stocks, ETFs do have expense ratios since they are managed, with a very wide range of the management fee across the ETF universe.

We have talked extensively about fees because even if expense ratios are small in some ETFs, the manager gets paid the expense ratio fee each year from your position no matter the performance, and it's often hard to see. Like mutual funds, you don't control which positions are bought and sold by the ETF fund manager, you are along for the ride. For many passive investors who don't want to try their hand with single stocks, ETFs are a very popular option.

The Takeaways: ETFs are seen by many as the evolved product from mutual funds. They are closed-ended like single stocks, but hold many stocks within each ETF. Their closed-end nature makes the performance easier to track in your account, and they can integrate well with your Stock Planting ™ system of tracking performance that you'll learn about shortly. They do have a wide range of fees, and you have no control over which stocks are bought and sold within the ETF.

Single Stocks Pros

With Single company Stocks, you have ultimate control of what to buy, when to buy, and when to sell shares. There is no expense ratio to owning stocks as you are the fund manager. Many brokerages now offer zero commission trades, and you can concentrate your portfolio in a way that is completely unique to you and at your comfort level. The longer your time horizon and holding period with single stocks, although there is no guarantee, you can tilt the odds in your favor of outperforming some of the best-run funds in the world. There are some single stocks that have gone up thousands of percent, trouncing the market over medium and especially long time periods. However good or bad your returns with single stocks, you will feel a unique sense of ownership. You have no one to blame or congratulate but yourself and your combination of luck, skill, and patience as an investor.

Single Stock Cons

That wonderful power of concentration that can work for you when companies' stocks are doing well, can overly hammer your portfolio when you're concentrated in a position that gets punished by the market. Your portfolio may fall much farther percentagewise than the overall market in a bad day, month, year or even years. As Chris Hill, former *Motley Fool Money* podcast host said, "This is the price of admission of being a single stock investor."

Many investors struggle to pay that price and remain true to their system during hard times, which is part of the reason I went to the work of writing this book for you, to encourage you to keep going! You may feel like a genius or an idiot, depending on the month or year, and how you've performed against the market with your single stocks. Don't forget to account for the likely high amount of randomness and luck in your investing success, this should help take some pressure off. The good news is you're probably not as smart or as dumb as you think! The important thing is to always keep investing, and by setting yourself up with your rules-based Stock Planting ™ system that you're about to learn, you will keep your cool when the high or low swings hit your account and positions.

The Takeaways: Owning shares of single stocks that you have picked can be incredibly empowering yet can feel a bit scary at first. The longer you do it, the more comfortable you'll get, which is why I encourage starting small. It can be an emotional roller coaster, but learning to ride the ups and downs can be very rewarding both emotionally and financially for the patient investor.

CHAPTER 6: WHY TRY TO BEAT THE MARKET?

We have likely all heard at some point some version of the statistic that 85% of active managers fail to beat the stock market average return over time. While most do not beat the market, some can and do. I am not predicting that because of reading this book you will beat the market, but after shoring up your personal finances as described above, you can begin to build a stock picking system, I dubbed Stock Planting ^{TM}, that gives you a chance. This system can help you worry less about things you can't control with investing, focus on what you can control, and tilt the odds in your favor of outperforming the market.

Investing in nearly any asset class is in a sense speculating, as no one can predict the future. Just because others have made or lost money on varying stocks, does not mean you will. Historical data only gets us so far when looking into the future, there are just so many unknowns. You must be okay with a small or large portion of your investing success being attributed to luck. While luck does play a role, skill in stock selection and patience to hold good companies' stock for long periods of time shouldn't be discounted either. The stock market, especially for single stock investors, has a way of keeping us excited yet humble. You'll ride the highest highs, enjoying single day gains of boast worthy 10, 20% or 30%+ in positions you hold, and you begin to think it was your genius that led you to it, your hindsight bias telling you that you "knew" this stock was undervalued and sure to have its day in the sun soon.

Just when you think you've discovered another, similar "can't-miss" stock to the first one that did so well, you watch your new stock plummet 20 or 30% right after you purchase it and wonder why you got into stock picking at all! The emotional roller coaster that comes along with single stock investing cannot be understated, which is why many people simply aren't cut out for it.

For those who are or at least think they are cut out for it, I want to give you a new way to think about stock picking. This system will help you develop your own framework for what companies to buy, how much of the company stock to buy, when to buy them, and when to sell. This system can help curb (never fully eliminate unfortunately!) the impulse to act (sell or buy) without a logic-based system in place. I want to help you build a system ahead of time and make rules for yourself. Doing so in advance will give you the advantage so that when you see the large emotional moves in the market, you'll be able to better stick with your system, and ignore the short-term hype or doom.

The takeaways: Performing better than the stock market averages is tough, most can't do it. Single stock investing is one of the ways you could outperform, but it takes the right temperament, skill, some luck, and a solid plan that you'll actually stick to. High highs and low lows are part of the game if you choose to invest this way, but you have some unique advantages as an individual investor.

Advantages of Being the Little Guy

Why be a single stock investor at all? How could you possibly compete against the many well-funded, well-pedigreed, sophisticated institutional fund managers out there? Well, again, while I can't promise you'll outperform them or even the general market by selecting your own stocks, I do want to point out a few distinct advantages small retail investors like us can have. You can think of them as your secret superpowers of investing.

Time Horizon

We'll get into your personalized time horizon or holding period later in the book, but I want to mention at this point the difference between expectations placed on fund managers and those placed on you. We've already discussed that any accounts you invest in with single stocks should not be something you're saving for the short term. Before investing you should first insulate your financial life with lower consumer debt and more cash savings to prevent as much as possible the need for you to access the stocks in an emergency.

Besides you and maybe your spouse or significant other, no one else cares or is checking in on your stock performance quarter to quarter, year to year, or even decade to decade. This anonymity can free you up to stick to your plan despite short-term market gyrations. Fund managers and investment companies, on the other hand, are scrutinized for their performance year to year heavily, and even quarter to quarter, possibly month to month in some cases. These managers are often investing with millions or billions of dollars of other people's money, after all. Although not a predictor of failure in any sense, this shortened time horizon must certainly be a factor in the fund manager's decisions. While of course they want their fund to perform well, they may be less inclined to take risks, even when they have high conviction on certain holdings. If they are wrong on some big picks over the course of quarters or years, this could be devastating to them personally in their career, as their investors may not have unlimited patience. You, on the other hand, are free to invest as you please.

While I do recommend calculating your annual account and portfolio performance and comparing the 12-month return (net of any additions or withdrawals) against large market benchmarks such as the S&P 500 or another you choose, please don't give up if after a year or two you have underperformed. Remember, we're in this for the long term, and I hope you give your strategy at least a 5-year chance, if not much more, to measure your investing success. Remember, especially as you start your investing journey, generally your stock picking is not a large portion of your portfolio. You should have built that financial foundation of cash through savings accounts and broad based market funds through your 401(k) plan or IRA as a large portion of your portfolio, so even if you're underperforming in your single stock account for a while, you should be capturing those baseline market returns through your 401(k) plan or IRA so you're not "missing out" on the market returns while you work your way into building up the single stock portion of your portfolio.

The Takeaways: Being a small retail investor is incredibly liberating, you don't have anyone concerned about your quarterly, yearly, or even multi-year returns, except you. You can research and buy nearly any stocks you want, and can start small with single stocks, matching the market with your other funds as you work into your single stock portfolio.

Portfolio Concentration

We will get into more details later on portfolio concentration both by account and total portfolio, but one of the advantages you have as a retail investor is you can concentrate your portfolio however you'd like. Many mutual fund managers are limited to 5% of their entire portfolio in any single stock position, to be more conservative and spread out the fund risk. This makes sense when they are dealing with large funds designed for millions of investors. Their goals are usually trying to either outperform the market by a small margin, keep level with the market, or underperform the market as little as possible. This conservatism also stems from their fear of the returns of the portfolio being dragged down over the short term if a concentrated single position underperforms. This could risk upsetting investors in their fund and possibly dealing with investors pulling their money from the fund over a bad short-term loss. My point here is not to rag on fund managers, they have extremely tough jobs and most do excellent work, but to point out that as a retail investor, you're not held up by many of these limitations.

You, on the other hand, can be as concentrated or spread out as you want in your portfolio, and have no investing board or potentially emotional clients to answer to if your performance in the short-term is lackluster. The only emotional investor you have to deal with is yourself!

Although I like to work my way into concentrated positions which I will detail in subsequent chapters, I found out after a year or two of picking stocks, that too much portfolio dilution turned out to have a negative outcome for my accounts. I did not have enough concentration in any of my single stock holdings, which did not allow any of my big winners to add any significant gain to my overall portfolio when they did do well. I was so timid of being wrong and over-concentrating in any one position, I had nearly no concentration at all. As an example, even a

50% one-day gain in a stock that is only 0.2% of your whole investment account makes a nearly negligible difference. This will be different for each person, but eventually you will want to work toward a level of concentration in your portfolio to be able to see appreciable gains in your accounts when your winning stocks continue to win.

The Takeaways: You can be as concentrated or diluted as you want in your positions, you don't have to follow anyone else's mandate. Starting small and adding more concentrated positions over time is a key element to the Stock Planting ™ system, I'll show you how it works very soon!

Small Company Investability

Another advantage individual investors have over certain large funds or investment companies is the ability to invest in small companies. While I believe you should invest in a wide range of sizes of companies large and small, and by company size I refer to the section that will follow on Market Cap, many large investment companies are limited to buying shares of only medium to larger companies. The reason is that their fund holds so many hundreds of millions or even billions of dollars.

As an example, if the very large fund manager takes even a small allocation to a very small company worth only a few hundred million or so, they will immediately own such a massive stake in the company as to either become a majority owner or could buy the company outright, which is not what most fund managers are attempting to do. In addition, it may be such a small percentage of their own total fund portfolio as to make a negligible difference in their total returns even if that small stock outperforms. It could also make it tough to withdraw their massive fund position without sinking the stock since they would own such an outsized stake, so it's often not worth it for the large fund. Many are restricted to buying only the largest, most liquid stocks. But you, on the other hand, can buy a single share or even a fraction of a share for a starter position, and it will not make market waves or headlines. In fact, no one will notice or care, except you! Some of your positions in smaller companies may become some of your biggest winners, and long before large funds will even be able to look at them.

Truly Open Market

The last advantage you have is some of the best fund managers may not be able to invest in certain holdings due to company compliance rules, the branding or political optics of holding certain public companies, or many other non-investing reasons. You, unless you work for one of these companies, are not limited, and can buy, hold, and sell whatever positions you'd like, it is truly an open market to you. There is typically less paperwork and lower fees for you to invest as an individual investor, and most investing platforms now offer zero commission for buying or selling stocks and ETFs. This has improved drastically in the past decades for retail investors.

You will often pay a very small fee called a spread, the difference between the bid and the asking price of the stock when you purchase a stock, but this should not discourage you from purchasing, it is usually a minutely small percentage that you pay only when you buy or sell. The longer your holding period, the more miniscule this spread is, it most affects day-traders who move frequently in and out of positions.

There are many myths about investing in single stocks, and I hope to break many of them in this book, but one that has always bothered me is "if you are buying a stock, that means someone is selling that stock". The intonation of this quote is you don't know what the other guy knows that you don't, which is causing him to sell and you to buy. I find it overly pessimistic. First off, everyone invests differently for different reasons, at different times in their life or career, based on their own needs or goals, so I don't believe we should unduly worry about that point.

Second, while there is market matching that occurs, that is matching up a stock buyer with a seller, this does not always happen. There are individuals called market makers or specialists, whose job it is to provide liquidity, or available shares, to the market. They do this by buying up large tranches of stocks, bonds, and ETFs, and selling or buying them when investment orders are placed. That spread I mentioned earlier is the small commission or markup that they get for providing the stocks to sell or to purchase. So, the other person buying or selling that stock to you may or may not have a reason to buy or sell, other than to help facilitate the trade to keep the market system moving and make a small profit of their own. The shorter your investing time horizon, as in day-trading, the more the spread matters, the longer your time horizon, holding the positions for years if not decades, the less.

The Takeaways: You can invest in small and large companies, without worrying about making waves in the stock price. No one is looking over your shoulder telling you which shares you can't buy, it is truly an open market for you. The cost of buying single stocks has decreased dramatically in the past decade, and the longer your holding period, the more negligible the trading costs.

PART II - THE FOUR PHASES OF STOCK PLANTING

We're finally here. You've been patiently waiting to get to the actual stock picking strategies through the introduction, foundation, and account type sections of the book, and we've now arrived at the meat and potatoes of the book, Stock Planting ™. I want to start by discussing the four levels of buying and selling stocks. I have developed these steps through the school of hard knocks; I think early on I made nearly every investing mistake possible when it came to single stock investing. I have learned, refined, and put into practice this strategy over the course of years, and am beyond excited to share it with you. It can help you start thinking about how to develop your own strategies, and how you would tactically implement them. First is the Watchlist Phase, second is the Seed Phase, third is the Nurturing Phase, and fourth is the Trimming Phase.

CHAPTER 7: PHASE 1 - THE WATCHLIST PHASE

What is a watchlist? Why should I build one? As of the writing of this book there are over 3,000 publicly traded companies domestically in the USA. There are even more abroad. How do you know which companies you should invest in? It can feel overwhelming at first, especially if you've never bought a single common stock share before. I recommend starting something like a spreadsheet or table to track the companies you are interested in, to help you stay organized. At first, I tried to do this only on my phone on a notes page, but it quickly became a huge mess. After a couple of months, I couldn't remember the company names, or tickers, or why I was even interested in investing in them. A watchlist both helps organize and helps you sort by priority some of the stocks you're most excited about investing in, both in the near term and longer term. On the spreadsheet or table, you can come up with your own labeling system that you may tweak over time, but here are a few distinguishing labels I found useful, there are 5 in total. Stock Ticker, Company Name, Market Cap, Stock Source, and the Investing Thesis.

Stock Ticker

This is the labeling system for publicly traded companies. Each company has its own Ticker, usually 1-4 letters, mutual funds often have 5. They are sometimes but not always abbreviations of the company names, so it is good to write down both the ticker and the name. You will usually need to enter the exact ticker when placing an order for a stock, so make sure you double check that the company you want to buy is correlated to the ticker you enter. There have been notable examples of investors rushing into what they thought was the ticker of a company they wanted to buy because it most closely resembled what they thought it should be phonetically, and they only found out later it was a company with the same name but in a completely different industry. What we're building isn't the type of investing system that you should rush into in any case, but it's important to stay organized.

Company Name

This one's obvious, no need for much comment here, but it is helpful to stay organized and distinguish this from the Ticker.

Market Cap

The Market Capitalization (Market Cap for short) is the size of any publicly traded company. This is simply the number of shares outstanding multiplied by the current stock price. The Market Cap is the right way to compare company sizes against each other, not the current stock price. Many investors get focused on the current dollar price of a single share of a company and compare it against others, but the actual price doesn't mean as much as the market capitalization, except for stocks trading for under $5.00. These are called pink slip stocks, or over the counter stocks (OTC), and you may want to exercise caution and do extra research before investing in companies with this low a price, as they are typically tiny companies either just starting out, or almost completely decimated from former highs.

New investors can incorrectly make the assumptive leap that a cheaper stock price means the company has much more room to grow than a stock with a higher price. This may or may not be true. A low priced stock price can go from a few dollars down to a few pennies and never come up, and a stock priced at hundreds or thousands of dollars per share may rise to many more hundreds or even thousands more in the future. Stocks move in percentage changes, not dollar amounts; this can be hard to remember when everyone talks about share price in dollars so often.

The market capitalization of a company is useful to compare against other companies, to see its relative size. Often a small company is one that has a market cap of under $2 billion, especially under $1 billion. These are typically newer companies, but not always. Some older companies' stock price declines over decades as the business slumps and they find themselves down there as well. Others under the $2 billion Market Cap can be good companies, but haven't yet found traction with the public, even if they have been around for years.

A medium sized company would fall between 2 and 10 billion, and 10 billion and up are large market cap companies. Currently market caps can go anywhere from a hundred million or so all the way up to currently over 2 trillion, which is a tough number to conceptualize. I know this market cap number will change somewhat by the time you purchase the stock vs when it goes on your watchlist, don't worry about that, you can always check the market cap on the day you buy a share or fractional share if you'd like. The point is to see the bigger picture of the size of the company relative to some others on your list to see what size mix of companies you're buying.

When diversification is discussed, it is often mentioned regarding buying companies from different industries or sectors of the economy to spread out your risk and increase the chances of positive returns. This is good advice, but it is also good to think about diversifying over a large range of market capitalizations as well, as companies' stocks within different market capitalizations can perform quite differently, too.

Stock Source

I added the Stock Source, or how I heard about the stock, after some time utilizing a watchlist. As my watchlist grew, even if I had a good thesis for investing, (which is the next item on the watchlist), I found if I didn't have the context to link the thesis of investment to how I discovered the company, I had a hard time weighing the varying excitement level I had about the companies to invest in, as certain sources have been more credible for me than others. If you choose to omit this watchlist category or add other categories I don't mention, no problem. This whole list should be personalized to you and how your brain best organizes and remembers information.

The internet has made the accessibility of instant access to information so easy. So much so, that it can become easy to become overwhelmed and not know where to start. There are so many resources you can use to build out your watchlist, and as I mention below, it will likely change over time as you become a more comfortable investor. Famous stock picker and fund manager Peter Lynch, in his book *One Up on Wall Street*, describes that your sources for your watchlist can come from everywhere around you.

He mentions a few examples such as: industries you work or have worked in and are familiar with, products or services you hear about from friends or family, local companies in your community that are publicly traded, or products or services you personally use regularly and find distinguished among competing products or services. As you interact with all these products and services, start thinking, "I wonder what company makes/provides this? Are they a publicly traded company?" I would add online articles, podcasts, books, even television shows. Stock picking services are worth a mention as well, those can sometimes be helpful for those starting out not knowing where to begin.

There are many people out there with very different investing ideas, so take each one with its appropriate grain of salt. This is why I find listing the source of how I heard about a stock helpful. Even very smart people can be very wrong about a stock's future potential, over the short and long term. It is just so hard, near impossible, to guess all the future factors that will affect a company's stock, which is why systematizing your stock buying and selling with small starter positions can be so helpful, as we'll explore in the Seed Phase.

Please view every one of these sources as introducing you to a potential, but not promised, future investment for you. Please do your own research, as much or as little as fits your situation, interests, and time, before building out a watchlist of companies with a thesis of why you think the companies would make good investments.

Get good ideas from everyone, but you are the ultimate decider; it is your hard-earned money, your future financial freedom, it should matter most to you. Review your watchlist monthly, quarterly, semiannually, or annually, to see if any of your own "recommendations" to yourself get any more or less attractive as you continue to learn.

Thesis

I saved the most important item on the watchlist for last, and this is your investing thesis. This is your reason or reasons for investing in a company. We all hope our investments go up in value, or we would never invest.

If you don't have any thesis or belief that a company has a reasonable chance of performing well in the future, even if that future is a few years or a decade out, then don't buy it; you may be better off in that case sticking to buying low-cost index funds as described previously in the foundation section. This thesis, or reason for purchasing the stock, should be your own. What it signals is that you found something compelling enough in your research, however thorough or brief, to have conviction enough to circle back to this company later when you're ready to re-examine and buy it. You can get investing ideas from so many sources as described above, but the decision to buy is ultimately in your hands. When you add a company to your watchlist, it should help take some pressure off that you don't have to buy it immediately and may never actually buy it; it may be moved lower down on your watchlist as other companies you find seem more attractive options than this one.

Some companies will excite you with new industry innovation or new revenue growth opportunities. Others will excite you at their impressive cash-generating business model or defensive moat that may make it difficult for others to compete. Some companies will excite you for the newness and flashiness of the company, while on the other end of the spectrum others will excite you with the generational oldness of the company and solid ability to innovate and weather the changing market conditions over the decades or even century. Lastly, there are some companies that may be compelling simply because they aren't mainstream, you feel like you've found a company as Peter Lynch describes, "before Wall Street", as it seems like a very solid company but has few to no analysts following it.

There are two books I really liked that helped me think differently about the excitement of investing in new technology companies and opposite but not opposing that view, the excitement of what many consider the dull and (relatively unknown to investors) manufacturing industries. These get much less attention but are no less exciting in their own way.

The first book is *Nothing but Net* by Mark Mahaney, which goes through some great ways to think about evaluating new technology companies. The second is *The Titanium Economy* by Asutosh Padhi, Gaurob Batra, and Nick Santhanam. They go over the overlooked and very investable manufacturing economy in the US, and how technology innovation in many of these companies is alive and well. There are of course many other great resources out there, these are just a couple to get you thinking.

Sort Order

Your watchlist will likely start small, but over the years you will be adding to it, possibly removing some companies from it. Create it however you'd like, but I found it useful to rank the companies by highest conviction to lowest, with the highest conviction stocks, the ones you're excited about the most for the long-term, being closest or at the top of the list and ready to buy next. The long-term must be emphasized here, I do not believe short-term stock buying and selling, or day trading, is appropriate for most investors: the odds are too stacked against you.

There are firms whose sole purpose it is to buy and sell ahead of your orders, to make money in the microseconds between stock orders and movements. While some individuals have had success in day trading with their own systems and philosophies, it is counter to my philosophy and I can't recommend it for most people, me included. It is nearly impossible to know how stocks will move over such a short time horizon. So, the stocks at the top of your watchlist should not be stocks you buy because you think they will go up the next day, week, or even month or quarter. Rather, due to your research, you buy because you believe the companies have some competitive advantages that will provide future earnings power and momentum to carry the stock higher over the coming years and even decades.

The Takeaways: A watchlist can help keep you organized both in the beginning and long-term with your Stock Planting ™. Compare companies based on Market Cap not share price, to weigh how large or small the companies are. Diversify among industries and Market Cap. Weigh your sources for new stock ideas by listing the Stock Source, and most importantly determine your Investing Thesis, or unique reason the companies you choose to invest in could do well – perhaps better than the market – in the future.

How Often to Update Your Watchlist

I have found it useful to make different sections within my watchlist, usually just by blank rows for white space. I pay the most attention to my top 10, or 10 stocks that I am most likely to buy next. I pay the least attention to the bottom 20-50% of my watchlist. I may never purchase those, and that is okay. I like to adjust my top 10 or top 20 stocks about once every other month, or less, it shouldn't take a lot of time.

These stocks are not set in stone, and the order can change at any time, it is completely yours to own. The time I pay most attention to my watchlist is when I have the monthly deposit in my investment account and am ready to purchase. I usually review my top 5 and top 10 stocks, possibly glance at my top 20, to make sure my sort order I had previously outlined is still how I'd like it to be. In other words, I'm excited and ready to add a very small starter position to the #1 on my list. If I'm more excited about a different company, that should be my #1 when I'm ready to purchase.

Don't sort the companies you want to buy via stock price, as you may fall into the trap of only buying companies with a lower stock price. I definitely made this mistake early on, and it was a price bias that ultimately did not help my early account performance. If you don't have enough saved to buy a whole first share for your starter position, simply wait until your monthly deposits have accrued enough cash to buy a share of your #1 pick. Remember I said this system requires a lot of patience? Alternatively, you can always open your investing accounts with a custodial company that allows partial or fractional share purchase, if you think that is a more appropriate system for you. Then you could open a smaller starter position with only a few dollars or even one dollar per share.

Returning to your watchlist, re-examining your thesis, and seeing if there has been any recent news that may affect your excitement about the top ideas doesn't need to take a lot of time, but is a good last-minute check. At least for me though, given my time horizon on how long I plan to hold the stock, last minute news rarely changes my opinion if I believe the company is a quality pick for the long term. If you have one of your quality top 5-10 stocks on your watchlist ready to buy and you see its stock price take a single day nosedive and you think it oversold, that could be a chance to move it up on your watchlist and purchase it next at a discount, you were going to buy it soon anyways. Exercise caution here though and try to understand why the price dropped so much, or like Peter Lynch said, "you may be trying to catch a falling knife". If something large has fundamentally changed in the company, it may have much further to fall. It could also just as easily have been a short-term overreaction by emotional investors with lofty expectations; predicting the short-term movement of stocks is just so hard.

I do like to go through about the top 50% of my watchlist once per year, to see if I still have the same convictions and in which order. This is time consuming and tedious, so I only do it once per year with a good movie playing in the background. As companies are purchased and moved off my watchlist and onto my "owned" list, the watchlist does change over time, so once per year seems right to me, after doing this for a few years. If you find there are companies on the bottom 50% of your watchlist that you think will never interest you now that you've learned more about investing and about yourself as an investor over the years, cut them loose and free up the mental space, delete them completely off your list. There are many hundreds of amazing publicly traded companies out there, your hard-earned dollars and mental energy should go to the ones you're most excited about.

CHAPTER 8: PHASE 2 - THE SEED PHASE

Hindsight Bias

The Seed Phase may be one of the more controversial sections of the book, but I have found it so incredibly useful and practical once I formulated it. You don't have to start with large (to you) concentrated dollar amounts in new positions you open to eventually be wildly successful owning some of those positions. One of the things that bothers me most about hearing about amazing single stock returns is how the hindsight bias is typically framed. It usually goes something like this:

"If you had only bought $10,000 of this stock 25 years ago, you'd be a millionaire today." While this person is usually right mathematically, it is the 20/20 hindsight vision and high dollar amount that is so frustrating to me when it is posed in this way. At the time, 25 years ago, or whatever their timeline, the market cap, stock price, and outlook of that company was likely much different from what it is today.

First, how would an investor have known about that stock at that time? Second, to most investors starting out, $10,000 or even $1,000 is a lot of money to invest in the market at all, let alone put it all on a single company. While stories like this can be exciting to get you thinking about the positive effects of compound interest and how that could work for you in your own portfolio, it can be so hard to know today which companies are most likely to provide you potentially market-beating returns over the next 10, 20 or 30 years. This is why you can start with many small positions and work your way into them, and still have the potential to concentrate later to capture some of those large returns. You won't "miss out" or be "too late" on large winners, the runway for great stocks to compound massively is often far longer than most investors think.

The takeaways: It is okay to start with a single share or a fractional share as a starter position, you likely have much more time than you think to benefit from the stocks continued growth. You can add more shares later and keep growing your position once the stock has done well. By using this approach, you won't invest massively in stocks that go straight down for you, as some inevitably will despite great research. Let go of what you "could have made" with big investments in the past and focus on patiently looking forward at what you "can make" with enough time and the right system.

Acceptance of What You Can and Can't Control is a Superpower

The funny thing that I've learned about single stock investing is there are so many factors out of your control in how a company's stock will perform. You can do hours and weeks of analysis before buying a stock, read dozens of articles, read annual company reports, listen to quarterly company reporting calls (all of which can be useful activities), and still buy a stock that turns out to be a complete dud for you, even over the medium or long-term.

I wish I could remember who I heard it from, but I heard an analyst once say that a stock's price movement in a given day, quarter, year, or even multiple years can be roughly attributed to the rule of thirds. One third of the movement could be due to the <u>company</u> performance or investor sentiment about that specific company, one third due to the <u>industry</u> performance or investor sentiment about that industry, and one third due to the overall <u>total market</u> performance or investor sentiment about the stock market for that given period. (For the last one think bull (growing) or bear (declining) market). Perhaps the most impactful of the 3 is the individual company performance, but the other two do play a part in a stock's movement and it often goes undiscussed.

This rule of thirds is of course overly simple and won't be true in some cases, but I like this way of thinking. It shows that even if a company's fundamentals are sound, even if they are: producing free cash flow and making a profit, have amazing increasing revenue, customer retention, innovative leaps in their research and development, or any other positive improvement, their industry sector or the total market underperformance could drag them down in the short or medium term. Vice versa, mediocre companies can be temporarily boosted by a rising industry or raging bull market that seems to lift all tides, at least for a while.

This doesn't mean there was anything wrong with your

investment analysis, these company attributes can be great research starting points and part of your thesis for investment in some cases, give yourself some grace. It just points to the fact that much of a company's stock price movement is out of your and even the company's control. We as humans love to feel in control, and it can be hard to accept that there could be many unknowns in a stock's price in the future. There are many investors and analysts who dial in very deeply with a company's historical performance, financials, and company outlook etc. While these are important metrics, it doesn't always mean a company's stock will outperform the market or even perform well, you just don't know, and this can be hard to accept.

As an example, there are some companies stock I have bought because all the classic financial indicators said they were undervalued, which should have meant that over the medium and long term the market would recognize their intrinsic worth and their stocks would outperform. To my dismay, their stock prices remained the "undervalued" duds where I found them, even many years later.

There are other companies stock I bought which had "overvalued" fundamentals and many analyst indicators said the stock was surely ready for a brutal drop, that they must be very overvalued with high price to earnings ratios, among other metrics. Yet frustratingly for some of those analysts pronouncing doom upon the stocks, they rose and rose over the years. There were pullbacks along the way to the cheers of the bear investors, but thanks to many factors, the winners kept on winning. Others were eventually knocked down in price, not all winners win forever. And not all undervalued stocks stay that way forever, but the classic market valuation theory doesn't always apply.

I'm not trying to say these fundamentals aren't important, especially over the longer-term, but they aren't always the immutable predictors you'd think they would be in a stock's movement. If you waited for all stocks to become undervalued before buying, you could be leaving some winners who have so much room to keep winning out of your portfolio, indefinitely. If you only bought "undervalued" stocks you could find yourself lagging the market for years, it is great to have a mix of both types.

It is easy to think that because a stock has had a fantastic run, you missed out, it must be due for a big correction, but that is not always the case. Some stocks with great underlying businesses that have returned hundreds of percent gain over years, go on to return thousands or even tens of thousands of percent more gain after that, as hard as it can be to believe. You could have bought the stock at many "overvalued" points along the way, and still made a fantastic return.

The Takeaways: Giving up control is tough. Surrendering to the fact that much of a stock's future price movement is out of your predictive control can be even tougher. Buying small amounts of quality companies' stock at first and waiting for your thesis to be proved right or wrong over the years by the future stock performance can help you stop stressing about market moves that you can't control anyways. Undervalued stocks may eventually prove their value and become correctly valued with stock rises. They may also remain undervalued indefinitely with very poor stock performance. Overvalued stocks may prove they got ahead of themselves and correct massively, or they may keep rising to increasingly new heights. Accepting what you can and can't control in investing can give you peace of mind, and can become one of your investing superpowers.

Over-Applying Logic to an Often-Illogical System

The stock market is evaluated and invested in by rational, logical people and yet often those same investors act illogically, emotionally, or downright strangely during varying market conditions. It's humbling to realize how much of investing is out of your control, and this is exactly why so many investors have a hard time with it. There is no guarantee that buying single stocks will outperform the market, but I believe by following a set system you've created ahead of time, it can tilt the odds in your favor, especially over the longer term. The first half of the challenge is understanding how the stock market works under varying conditions; the second half of the challenge is understanding your own behavior and how you may act under different market conditions. I want to teach you how to set guardrails ahead of time to curb that emotional, often destructive behavior.

For all these reasons discussed, the Seed Phase is best described as once you have built even a rough sketch of your watchlist, you begin finally purchasing single shares of common stock. I call it the Seed Phase because to begin you will only purchase a single share of a company you want to invest in, or a fractional share if the share price of a single share is too high for you to reasonably save for over a period of time.

Skin in the Game

This Stock Seed, an extremely small starter position, (one share or a fraction of a share) may seem counterintuitive to my earlier reference about how only a concentrated portfolio has a chance to produce real results and outperform the market. But since you really don't know which of your stocks will be your winners in the beginning, you don't yet know which stocks you should concentrate your investing dollars into, right? Just because certain stocks have been winners or losers for others, doesn't mean they will be for you.

There is something very powerful about having skin in the game: your portfolio matters most to you. I can promise you this; you don't care as much about how much a company's stock has gone up or down if you haven't been participating. You feel jealous when you hear of others' massive investing success, and perhaps vindicated later when you hear of massive losses in those same positions you were previously jealous of. As robust as your watchlist may be, it will never be as important to you as the investments you have actually committed real dollars to, even if it's very few dollars at first.

The moment you buy your first single stock share, you start to care. Moving from the watchlist phase to the seed phase, you start to pay more attention to the companies because you have real dollars invested in them, however great or small. So, the big takeaway for the seed phase is to only open a new position in a company you've never invested in previously with a single share, no more. It must prove itself through percentage gain in your portfolio, worthy of re-purchases.

If you over-concentrate early on in just a few holdings, you may get lucky and pick a fantastic winner. If so, congrats. But maybe you don't get lucky with those concentrated holdings, it could be a big risk. If any of these very concentrated holdings take a massive dive and never recover, the emotional loss you feel could lead you to act rashly and bail out. You could sell too early from that or other positions because the loss had a more significant impact on your portfolio and on your emotional state, than if you had more widely spread out your investing dollars at first. You could become disillusioned with investing and leave the market for a while or indefinitely as some do after large losses in concentrated portfolios, depriving themselves of future wealth growth. That is the danger with early over-concentration.

A farmer doesn't expect every single seed he plants to grow into a crop. While it would be nice, he is being realistic with his chances, and spreads many seeds to start with, knowing some will die, but many will go on to grow well. In an absurd example of concentration, he doesn't plant just a few seeds, giving them the concentrated fertilizer of an entire acre's worth of crops, hoping those few plants will produce an outsized crop yield. This would likely kill the tiny crop and discourage or bankrupt the farmer.

Buying many stock seeds allows you to increase the probability that you've landed on one or hopefully a handful of companies that go on to fantastic heights. As we will learn in the Nurturing Phase, you'll have been adding to those winners steadily along the way with your unique, customized Stock Planting ™ system, and not adding any more to the stocks that only go down.

The Takeaways: Other people's investments and even your awesome watchlist will never matter as much to you as the investments you make with real money of your own. You'll move from interested to committed, even if it's a very small commitment. Take the first step, buy small, single positions or fractional positions of a mix of great companies, and your own Stock Planting ™ system will tell you how and when to buy more.

Whole Shares vs Fractional

This has already been mentioned a few times throughout the book, but I want to revisit it briefly. There are two ways to purchase single stocks in your brokerage or retirement account. You can buy whole shares or fractional shares, or a combination of the two. If you are utilizing fractional shares, you can open multiple smaller positions with an equal weight, or equal starting dollar amount.

There are pros and cons of starting with whole shares or partial shares. If you can save enough each month starting out to buy whole shares, you get the benefit of receiving the entire dividend (if applicable) payable to you each quarter and year. Also, if you ever want to switch brokerage companies (called custodians) where your account is held but want to hold on to your shares in the transfer, you can do so with full shares, but many brokerage companies will not transfer partial or fractional shares. They will make you liquidate (sell) the partial shares and transfer them as cash, locking in your gains or losses on those positions and making you restart that portion of your portfolio.

The downside of buying whole shares is your portfolio will start out, to not have a better word for it, somewhat lumpy. This is due to the large variance of the share prices of the respective companies on your watchlist. Prices can range from a few dollars to up to thousands per share, so you could either be left out of some of the largest priced companies or be forced to save for a significant amount of time to purchase a single share, depending on the amount you're able to contribute to your account monthly and which company stocks you purchase.

Once you do save up for those larger companies and purchase your first share, they will immediately become a larger percent of your total account than the smaller priced share holdings. This is neither a good nor bad thing, but it is something to consider. If you are going the path of the whole shares, just know that unless you have a lump sum to start investing, it will just take more time to build out your first group of starter or seed positions, maybe even a year or more, depending on how much you're able to deposit to your investing account or accounts each month. Once you start to re-buy shares of existing positions, it gets easier to get your whole share positions more in line with the other winners in your portfolio, so your portfolio won't be "lumpy" forever. Using whole shares is neither a better nor worse strategy than fractional shares, either will work well in this system, it all depends on your situation.

If you are just starting out and can't find very much in your budget each month to start investing in single stocks, fractional shares can be a great way to go, you can often purchase a fractional share of stock for as little as $5 or even $1 depending on the custodian. Even if you could afford to buy regular whole shares of companies, the fractional approach may appeal to you more. You can purchase a set dollar amount of each of your new stocks, and they will have what David Gardner calls "a fair starting line."

I'm paraphrasing now, but he goes on to say as soon as you purchase the fractional shares in the various companies, they will begin to sort themselves in your portfolio, as company stocks move quite differently from each other every day.

The Takeaways: Determine which approach, the whole share or fractional share method, fits better with your situation. Either can work great with the Stock Planting ™ system, but each has its limitations and benefits. A quick online search can show you which custodial brokerage companies permit fractional share investing if that route appeals to you more.

How many Stocks Should I Hold?

One question you may be thinking is, "How many stocks should you start with before adding to existing positions?" A follow-up is "How many stocks is too few, or too many?" As with this entire process, this will be personal to each investor. The *Motley Fool*, a popular stock picking and stock analysis service, recommends a portfolio of 20-25 stocks to start out with, before adding to existing positions. Some of you may be comfortable starting with 10, and others may feel they need 50+. I think any of these can be a great starting point, but I don't believe you need to cut yourself off at any certain number, especially with the way I advocate starting out, buying only a single share at first, or a fractional share.

Many investors advocate for just a few stocks, so you can really keep up with the research and news on each one of the companies and have more concentrated gains right away. This is probably a controversial point, but my own experience has been that loads of research on a few stocks hasn't really yielded better results than minimal research on many stocks. It isn't laziness, but rather an observation from my earlier days investing. After purchasing a seed share of a quality company, all my research activity trying to guess the future stock movements based on in-depth continued company analysis didn't really have an impact on my ability to predict the future share price movement.

As I stated previously in the rule of thirds, although a company's stock price movement does often return to the business fundamentals of the individual company, it is important to remember the other two thirds. There are many intangible factors within the industry, total market, and investor sentiment including reactions to financial reporting or company guidance that are emotional or momentum driven and are impossible to find on pages of detailed reports.

If people scoff at the idea of owning hundreds of individual stocks as too hard to keep up on, can anyone reading this book name more than 20 stocks of the S&P 500 index without looking them up? Are you keeping up weekly or monthly on the other 480 companies in the index that you can't rattle off? Me neither. Yet the Stock Planting ™ system I will describe is in a way like an index, where over time it will be self-selecting, and self-cleansing.

The losers, which you will not continue to add to, will become a smaller and smaller percentage of your portfolio as you add new monthly deposits to your account and these losing stocks keep going down. This will continue to the point where you truly don't care about their performance for the rest of your holding period unless the losing companies' stock dramatically improves. On the other end of the spectrum, your relatively few winners could boost the outstanding returns to carry your portfolio to new heights. You will inherently start to pay more attention to the businesses whose stocks become your winners, as they begin to make up a larger portion of your account over time. This is possible with the right investing framework, lots of patience, and some luck involved. You don't have to be a stock picking genius to win with this system, it is more akin to a continued expansion of your fishing net casting with small starts, patiently increasing your odds to land and add to a few whales.

The starting number of stocks you build up before adding more dollars to the original investments will be personal to you, but I do like the Motley Fool's recommendation of 20-25 stocks as a starting point. If you have at least a few hundred dollars per month to invest and choose the whole share method, building up to that could take you as long as a year or two, depending on the starting price of the shares you invest in.

If you can increase the dollar amount you invest monthly, you could reach your personal stock number much faster. Remember it's not a race, this is your journey, completely unique to you, no one's situation is the same. Everyone's financial situation is likely constantly changing, at least in small ways. Let go of the fear of missing out, there are dozens if not hundreds of great companies waiting for you to invest in them, that could be your big winners. I could have said the same thing 50 years ago and feel confident I will be able to say it again 50 years from now.

If you feel like you can't wait a year or more to build up your starting amount of stocks, or don't have a few hundred dollars per month to invest each month, the fractional share option may be the better starting route for you. Just remember that with tiny positions, come tiny dividends and tiny total returns. I hope everyone's starting point on funds available to invest each month, especially if it is small, does not remain that way forever.

The Takeaways: Determining how many single shares of stocks to start with before adding back to those you've already opened will be unique to each person. Find great companies and let them show you, through gain over time in your portfolio, that they are worth adding to, and in larger quantities. This book was purposely written without any calendar dates noted, as its principles could be applied many decades from now, no matter the "current" market conditions.

Pay Yourself Tomorrow

An idea from Tony Robbins' investing books mentioned earlier that I really liked was to "pay yourself tomorrow." The idea is that if you are honest with yourself and have a detailed monthly budget and truly don't have the monthly margin to start investing, then you will commit to yourself today to use a portion of any future raises, bonuses, or commissions to increase your savings rate in the future. That can take any guilt or shame away from your present inability to save and give you something great to look forward to. If you're worried about needing any raise to combat inflation, I also like the idea from Nick Maggiulli's book, *Just Keep Buying,* where he says it's okay to take half of any pay increase as lifestyle creep or inflation adjustment and promise the other half to your investing.

Meanwhile you could become a student of the market, reading many great books and articles on investing, and listening to podcasts about investing. You could be preparing your watchlist of companies you're excited to invest in, and possibly advancing in your career or educational or credential opportunities, which could give you that future possibility of more monthly investing dollars. This is part of the reason I wanted to start the book with building your financial foundation before jumping into investing. If you feel like you have no margin in your monthly income to invest but can pay off some or all of your consumer debt, those same dollars that you were paying to creditors, can now be utilized to build a more solid financial future for yourself.

The Takeaways: Even if you have no margin in your budget for monthly investing now, it doesn't have to stay that way forever. Promise a portion of future raises or even unexpected income to investing, and when you get there, the choice to invest is easier because you already made it ahead of time. Getting excited about future investing possibilities can spark positive changes in your life and career, to get you to the point you can invest regularly.

CHAPTER 9: PHASE 3 – THE NURTURING PHASE

Building on your Seed Phase

If you have been following along mentally in the book so far, let's imagine you have opened an investment account online through one of the brokerage companies that seem most suited to you.

Which account type that you choose to open is up to you, your situation, and goals. It could be a Roth IRA (my favorite), Traditional IRA, or a non-Qualified brokerage account (my second favorite).

You have pre-determined how many "seeds" or single shares of companies you will own, or if in the case of the fractional share route, how many partial shares of companies you will start with, before adding to any existing company stock you own. This will give you a starting point with a variety of companies' stocks, hopefully from a variety of industries and a variety of market caps (company size). Let the starting positions reflect what seem best to you.

You are likely champing at the bit to add to some of your better performing positions, for as soon as you started purchasing the shares, the performance among the stocks started to diverge. For the rest of the book I want to get away from focusing on the dollar amounts invested. Each person has a different situation, and focusing on the percentages makes the concepts more applicable to everyone. While some may have very little to invest at first, others, whether it be from an inheritance, high income, or a 401(k) plan from an old job that was rolled into a Traditional IRA or Roth IRA, the dollar values will be different for everyone.

What can make us all equivalent and can help you to craft your own personalized portfolio, is focusing on the percentages within your account. We talked at the beginning of the book about determining what percentage of your total portfolio could be made up by your single stock investments, that may eventually span multiple account types. This may change over the years as your investing comfortability, knowledge, and financial situation change, so we won't rehash it here. We will focus instead on the example of using a single account, for simplicity's sake.

I made the mistake early on in my stock picking journey of having a bad case of FOMO, or fear of missing out. I would hear stocks discussed - not even recommended - but just discussed on podcasts, or from news articles or books I read, even casually mentioned by friends and peers. I would want to buy the stocks immediately for the fear of missing out on possible great future gains. Especially if there had been some discussion of outperformance or even a slight differentiating factor with the way the company was run or in its mix of products or services, I would crave to be a shareholder as quickly as I could, because I felt I was missing out on all this "growth".

I accumulated many low-quality companies very quickly in this way, because I always felt I was missing "the next big stock", and if I just purchased it, I would participate in some of those great gains mentioned. In hindsight, while this has taught me many valuable lessons about the stock market, company selection, and lessons about myself and my ego, I would not recommend this path.

I lost what was to me at the time a lot of money, chasing purely speculative stocks and selling them quickly when they predictably didn't perform well in the short term. It was very frustrating. In addition, because I had a single share position in so many stocks and never concentrated my portfolio out of the fear of losing money and only wanting more and more new stocks, any outperformance of individual companies resulted in no appreciable gain to my account, because my account was so diluted.

If this seems contrary to the advice given in the last section about making sure you have many stocks to start with, I wanted to show how I made these mistakes early on taking it to extremes buying many low-quality stocks in knee-jerk fashion with no plan on how to manage them, and it wasn't fun. I almost threw in the towel with single stock investing early on, but my mind loves systems, and I knew it was something I could figure out. So instead of giving up I kept learning, and slowly built the Stock Planting ™ system. I hope it will make more sense in this chapter as we learn about how and when to add to your existing positions, and how to concentrate your portfolio in a systematized manner that removes (most) if not all the emotion and indecision that can rack many investors faced with uncertainty.

The Takeaways: There are always more stocks out there to buy. No one is immune to FOMO with investing, but some have it worse than others. Recognizing the greener grass impulse within yourself can help you temper the emotion. Systematizing your approach can help even more, and you'll begin to see that some of the stocks you hold in your portfolio already, given the right timetable and parameters for re-purchase, may be just as good if not better than the new ones you're excited about on your watchlist.

Only Add to Your Winners

The first rule that I implement in adding to existing positions is, I only add to my winners. That is, I only purchase more shares in stocks that have gone up in value. The phrase "Add to your Winners" comes from famous investors like David Gardner and Peter Lynch, and I build more upon it with my own thoughts and process. I don't add to losing stocks - stocks that have a negative total return for me - no matter how promising I think the company is, or how undervalued it may seem, or even how many prior years of outperformance it may have had before I bought it.

Here we go for another controversial point! I only add to those stocks that show a positive total appreciation over time in my own portfolio, regardless of what they have done in the past for others or what current changes the company or stock market may be going through. I have heard this labeled in investing circles as "anchoring" to a price that only I am aware of, that the company and market does not know or care about what I paid for the stock, so I shouldn't either. The critics would be right, I am 100% anchoring to my own portfolio and the respective stock starting points within it, and I'm unafraid of the criticism this might bring. This anchoring permits me to not stress from that point on, the stock price movement is out of my control, and it's liberating.

I must return to my comment made previously; your portfolio matters most to you, more than anyone in the world. If a company stock that I research, add to my watchlist, get excited about, and finally pull the trigger and buy a single share immediately plummets over the months and years after I purchase it, then I don't sell it, but have deemed it not yet worthy of repurchase. While I will typically not sell it except under extreme circumstances, (more on that later), I will not buy more shares of the stock until it has risen back up into positive territory and maintained above a certain total return for a time.

It may sound somewhat silly to punish a formerly beloved

stock in this way. While the company fundamentals may seem good, and the stock may or may not have made money for other investors, it has not yet done so for me. This may seem completely illogical or even childish at first glance, but remember, you started out with seeds, not massive dollar amounts, and to paraphrase what investor Peter Lynch said, "...Don't water your weeds, water your flowers, (eventually) pull your weeds. Add to your winners."

What about the company now being even cheaper with a reduced share price? With my high conviction and research done into how great a company this may be, don't I want to buy even more shares? Not me. I have done this before, and while it has worked a few times, in more cases I have bought more shares of the companies and ended up adding to losers that never recovered into positive return territory even after many years. They still may recover, so I won't sell yet, as I haven't reached my personal holding period for the stocks I purchased, but I won't add more until the company stock performance shows me it merits more of my hard-earned investing dollars. I'm not saying this should or shouldn't be your rule, but it is one of mine, and it frees me up mentally and emotionally from agonizing about when or whether to add to a losing or declining stock.

Some investors do add to beaten down positions in companies they love, and if you choose to do that, it is your choice. I like finding high quality companies to start with, but I don't find myself good enough at predicting the future stock performance of any company to commit more hard-earned investing dollars to a stock that has dropped.

If the company is indeed undervalued, instead of re-purchasing now, a long enough holding time horizon of multiple years will let it earn itself a spot on my re-purchase list if it grows back into positive territory. You might argue that I am missing out on all the potential gains to be had in the gap between where the company share price is and the price I bought it, and I won't argue with you there, that is close to the very definition of this price anchoring I'm doing. But again, there is no guarantee it will come back up at all, I may have had the worst timing ever and bought the stock at the absolute peak for the next 10 years, even good companies can have lousy stock performances for long periods of time. If I was unlucky enough buy at a multi-year peak, then I won't waste any more dollars hoping that stock will surpass my initial buy-in point.

A company's financial health, products, services, management, and investor sentiment can change over time. With a long enough holding period, either that stock will eventually make its way back above my rebuy minimum or "Stock Nurture" threshold where I will happily buy more of it, or it will continue to wallow and get sold at the end of my holding period, with me the wiser for the lessons learned investing in it. I want to focus on the long-term, and it is not as improbable as you think for single stocks to recover dozens and hundreds of percents over years to boost themselves back into positive territory. You must recognize the flip side; it is also not improbable for some to never return to the previous apparently high price I started with.

If you're starting to feel overwhelmed with keeping up with some of the percentages and figures, not to worry, I will go through a couple of percentage examples at the end of the book, so you can get an idea of how to formulate your own "Stock Nurture" rebuy minimums, among some other key metrics to building your Stock Planting ^{TM} System.

The Takeaways: Only add to your winning stocks and be extremely slow to sell. Free yourself from the anxiety about what to do with a losing stock. Give the company time to figure things out but don't add more shares to the position while it's in negative territory for you. Slow down, relax. This is a long-term game where the patient investors are rewarded. Either the stock will eventually come back up and keep going up as you add more shares to it, or you'll be glad you didn't waste more money adding to a stock that doesn't come back.

A Tale of Two Public Companies

Before moving on to more tactical steps, I want to bolster a bit more the idea of how only buying companies that have gone up for you can make sense, with the right time horizon. I want to briefly visit the idea of a company's earnings, stock price momentum, and incentivized employees, through a made-up but not completely improbable story.

Many company employees of publicly traded companies, due to wonderful employee stock purchasing programs, have a large portion of their personal net worth tied up in the stock performance of the company they work for. As the quarters and years of their employment go by, and as the stock price rises, their personal net worth rises as well. If the employees in publicly traded companies are far removed from the stock market and investing, there is likely at least one company's share price they pay attention to on a weekly basis, and that is the company they work for, since it matters so much to their personal wealth.

If the stock falls, so does a portion - often a large portion - of their net worth as well. While almost all employees don't and shouldn't try to manipulate the stock price by their individual or department performance, you can imagine the excitement if the stock consistently grows over the years, and the renewed efforts these employees apply to their respective roles. Productivity likely goes up fueling earnings growth, employee retention likely improves, and the general mood of the company is probably full of optimism and excitement as the employees feel they are all "winning together" and want to do their part to continue to help the company succeed. Outsiders are attracted to the apparent success and possible stock options, and talent acquisition seems easier to get the best and brightest to come work for this successful company.

Now for a second company example. You can imagine if you were one of the employees of a company in which the stock price had once seen great heights, and your personal stake had seemed considerable and growing, so you never sold shares along the way. After years of poor performance, the stock has been punished, down 50% or more from its highs, and a sizable portion of your personal net worth along with it. While you try to put on a cheerful face and work hard to turn things around since you are being paid for your work, we can imagine the inevitable glum atmosphere each time the stock price takes a beating at the next poor quarterly result, and you begin wondering if now is the time to cash out and move on.

Of course, these two companies are fictional, (I'm sure there are several technical holes in my stories too), and the story is completely made up. But I hope you see the point about intrinsic company momentum, and how employees, investors, analysts, and the stock market love to give love to winning companies. Positive or negative momentum is as real in the business world as in the world of sports and other aspects of life. It is hard to describe with a spreadsheet, but very real. I like to add to my winners to participate in the long-term momentum of successful companies and wait to add to those whose stock prices have fallen on hard times, to find their momentum and turn it around. Some investors will try to time their opening position and only add new starter positions to companies that have 6 months or so of positive stock market price gains. While I think that's an interesting idea and speaks to the momentum discussed, it's not something I've strictly stuck to. I focus on the business and its advantages, and open extremely small starter positions and wait and see what happens.

Thoughts on Reallocation

I believe investors everywhere give weight to stocks that keep on winning, and the market rewards excellence and continued outperformance. Sometimes the market rewards these companies in the long term, sometimes only in the short term, but it does reward them. The idea of a stock being down 50% or more and recovering back into positive territory only seems crazy to those with a short time horizon, and those that haven't seen it happen in their own portfolio.

I've witnessed it a few times when company stocks get beaten down to a miserable level within my portfolio. A lot of patience and time has let those few quality companies figure out what wasn't working, make the right moves over time, and the market rewarded them and their shareholders for it. Why didn't I add to these companies on the way up? Because for each of these unique companies who do make it back into positive territory, there are 2 or 3 that don't, and their stocks wallow down at the -50% to -80% range for years. It can be so hard to tell the difference in the short term.

Why not sell the shares, wait 30 days (for what is called a wash rule), and re-buy the shares at the new lower price? This one is more psychology than math, as is much of this book. Mathematically that could make sense. But most investors who sell shares after a painful loss, telling themselves they will re-buy soon, rarely if ever re-purchase the stock later, waiting indefinitely on the sidelines with that company stock. They have been psychologically "burned" by the poor performance and pain of losing money associated with that stock, and the new lower price can't help but seem indefinitely "overvalued" to the wary investor.

I thought each of the companies in which I purchased a share had at the time a unique or compelling something. A unique or compelling story, product, service, defensive moat, leadership team, financial situation, etc. or I wouldn't have purchased a single share to begin with. But I don't have to invest additional dollars on beaten down companies' stock until the company proves themselves worth it. I like to focus on the business while researching companies to invest in, and less on the stock performance or hype. Even with lots of research, it can be so frustrating to believe so much in a company, yet watch the stock go nowhere for years. This is why I wanted to systematize my investing process.

Stock Planting ™ can work in all market conditions, as your portfolio is constantly self-sifting through winners and losers. In my experience, during "bull markets" (rising stock market conditions) I was able to concentrate and add shares to companies within my portfolio that were actually winning, not just those I believed could or should be winning, that's an important distinction. During "bear markets" (falling stock market conditions) there are large sweeping selloffs in which few if any of my companies' stock were above their rebuy minimum, so I wasn't able to add to as many existing winners during that time. This could seem like a negative situation for most investors, but not for me. I was able to open new seed positions of new companies from my watchlist and I watched and waited to see what grew.

Many investors fear buying at market tops, so they hold off on investing more in winning companies, selling their winners after a quick gain, to reallocate to some other stock that appears undervalued to them. While this is a great idea in theory, there are so many quality companies that appear with the "overvalued" label based on some seemingly sound financial principles yet go on to decades more of winning in company growth and stock appreciation, all while remaining "overvalued." The investors may have been better off keeping or adding to those winning positions instead of selling them.

There is a common idea of a quarterly or annual "rebalance" where investors and fund managers routinely sell winners, stocks or segments of stocks that have outperformed, ostensibly with the hope of buying new winners elsewhere. This practice in theory lets you take gains off the table from stocks that have grown "too much". However, buying new stocks is not guaranteed to give you better portfolio performance than the stocks you currently hold. This is why adding to existing positions that have met winning criteria for you can be so powerful. One of my favorite sayings about selling stocks that I agree with completely, is that if you sell one investment to buy another, you have to be talented enough to be right twice: you have to be right that the investment you sold will not go on to outperform after you've sold it, and you have to be right that the new investment will outperform the first. This is a tough task!

The Takeaways: Keep buying small shares of what you determine are quality companies with a competitive advantage, and only add to those companies whose stock has gone up for you. Be reluctant to add to quality companies with losing stocks, be eager to add to quality companies whose stock has gone up for you over time. Successfully selling winners to buy other perceived winners is very hard. Keep buying or holding those winners you have unless none are currently winning, the grass isn't always greener.

Systematize It

James Playsted Wood said, "The thing that most affects the stock market is everything." I love this quote because stocks can go up and down for so many reasons, many of which are unpredictable. Building yourself a system can help reduce the many attempts to apply rationality to an often-irrational market. It can remove some of the indecision and fear of buying and selling stocks. The longer you employ your system, making small tweaks to match your investing style even better over time, the more comfortable you will become as an investor.

I'm sure you're more than ready to get into some specific examples of this in practice, so here we go. I will use specific percentage numbers, but please remember these are examples only. I want you to think through these strategies and determine some good starting ranges and percentages for you, which may change over time.

Let's say for example you have 25 single shares spread across different industries and market caps, you have completed your initial Stock Planting ™ watchlist and the Seed Phase. Depending on if the market is in a bull or bear market while you were buying your starter seed positions, you may have many that are down from when you bought them, and only a few that are up, or many that are up and only a few that are down. Either way there is likely a larger dispersion than you thought there would be, that is part of the magic of single stocks. I have observed that stocks of even similar companies do not move nearly as much in lockstep as you would think.

For your stocks that have a positive total percent gain, you will begin to re-buy those stocks in a more concentrated way (more shares of fewer companies) that will be detailed shortly. For your stocks that are in negative territory, you still like the companies, but are not going to re-purchase any of them currently, not until they gain and return to positive territory. Before we move on to explain how to re-buy more shares of existing companies that you hold a share in, we need to distinguish your companies, as not all of them behave the same, and should not be treated the same. For simplicity, I have separated all stocks into 2 categories, Growth and Value, with Growth being stocks that don't pay a dividend, and Value being stocks that do. Before I get scolded that there are many value type stocks that don't pay a dividend, and there are some growth stocks that do, you're probably right, but this is my system to keep things simple, and it works for me. You may come up with a different way to distinguish your groups of stocks, and that is great.

Growth Vs Value

Remember that each company, if it is profitable, must decide what to do with the cash it generates from doing business. It can reinvest the cash in the company for improved equipment, personnel, or processes, or use it for acquisitions of other companies that complement its offerings. It could buy back some of its shares to increase earnings per share for each of its shareholders, it can hold the cash on its books against a rainy day called retained earnings, or it can return some of the cash to shareholders in the form of an annual, quarterly (most common) or monthly cash dividend.

The amount of dividend is a dollar amount per share that the company has decided for that period, typically it's an annual figure divided by the number of times in a year a company pays out the dividend. It applies to your account based on the number of shares you hold. If a company has decided not to pay a dividend, it typically believes a better use of its cash would be to reinvest the cash its own operations, pay down debt, acquire another company, or buy back shares. A share buy-back reduces the number of total shares outstanding, and makes your share or shares represent a larger portion of the net profit, in a metric called earnings per share.

When a company chooses not to pay a dividend, with the exception of share buy-backs, their non-dividend actions are usually seen as fueling growth activities. So, the primary form of benefit they expect to give to you, the shareholder, is in the form of company revenue growth, which hopefully leads to more earnings, thus more earnings per share, thus higher stock price appreciation. These are typically but not always companies in growth mode. Newer companies typically fall into the growth non-dividend paying camp, but not always. Many newer companies could not afford to pay a dividend even if they wanted to, as they are often borrowing money heavily to finance the company operations. As a growth investor you are along for the sometimes-wild ride of growth stock investing.

For Value companies that decide to pay a dividend, they are usually more established in their market. They are great at producing cash, and have decided as a way to reward shareholders, in addition to hopefully gaining stock price appreciation through growth activities, they pay some of the generated cash back to their shareholders as a dividend. Be wary of chasing dividend stocks only based on their yield, (the dividend percent of their share price that the company is paying you to hold the stock), you should still analyze the company for growth reasons as well.

Buy great companies for all of the right reasons listed previously and more importantly your own reasons you've come to through your own research. If the company happens to pay a dividend it is the icing on the cake of what we hope is a slower growing, but still growing company. I recognize for my newer investor readers that this section was very technical, if you didn't understand some of the terms, go back and re-read the section, looking up some of the terms for greater clarification if needed.

The Takeaways: Growth companies have decided the best way for shareholders to win with them is through purely growth activities that can accelerate the stock price, using earned cash for everything except paying a dividend. Value companies still attempt to grow in various ways, and some can be strong growers, but they have determined that a good use for a portion of their cash is to reward shareholders each year through a cash dividend. A good portfolio could have some of both types, Growth and Value, mixed in. The mix may change over time as the investor learns more about their own preferred investing style.

Rebuy Minimums

I am spending so much time on defining Growth Vs Value stocks because in the Stock Planting ™ system there are different rebuy minimums, or percentage gain thresholds that act as a signal to buy more shares, when moving from the Seed Phase to the Nurturing Phase for a company's stock. I split this up for companies that are to me either Value or Growth, by my determination of dividend-paying vs no dividend. For Growth companies, I expect their price to generally be much more volatile, with greater swings up and down, and so I have a higher positive minimum percentage that I want that company's return to be, before I buy more shares. Alternatively, for a Value (dividend paying) company I expect generally slower growth, so I have a lower minimum percentage that I rebuy shares for those companies. In this way all public companies fall into one of the two designations.

For some examples, you could think of re-buying shares of a Value company when it reaches a positive appreciation of +15%, maintained for a period of your choosing to eliminate single day price pops followed by sudden drops as the price surge is sold. The period for which its price must be maintained above your target (+15% in this example) could be 2-4 weeks, or any period you choose. For Growth stocks you could say it has to reach +30% total appreciation and maintain that level for the same period before re-buying. Or, you could say Value stocks, +20%, and Growth, +50%. The numbers and time period you wait before rebuying are completely up to you.

I know I'm repeating myself, but the longer you do this, the more you will get comfortable with which levels work for you. For me, at first, I didn't wait very long. The day I had the money in my investment account I re-bought shares of any appreciated stocks, and it didn't go super well for me. I added to stocks that were barely positive, and then after I re-bought they plummeted below 0%. As time has gone on, I've gotten more patient, I usually wait at least 2 weeks from when a stock passes its rebuy minimum level to re-buy, which usually corresponds with my bi-monthly deposits from my paychecks. I have also had to become more patient to save up to add to some positions, as my portfolio size has grown over the years, this is a good problem to have! That is why I said 2-4 weeks, some positions take a month or more to save up for. You will experience this as well the longer you work your system, even using fractional shares.

I would recommend trying to stick with your predetermined rebuy minimum levels to avoid a particular bias towards one of your favorite companies. Try to look at it from a level field and remain neutral, don't fall in love with any one stock. What is a stock darling for you today, could drop suddenly seemingly out of nowhere on you, it has happened to me many times. Only buy as your system dictates. Act as if you're managing the money for someone else, and not yourself, and remain focused on the percentages, not the dollar amounts.

Following the +20%, +50% example above, if I had a Growth stock (non-dividend) that had grown to +40%, it would be second in line to a Value stock (dividend payer) that had grown and held at +21%. I would re-buy the Value stock and need to wait until the Growth stock grew to 50%+ and held that level for a couple of weeks. The gap between Value and Growth rebuy minimums naturally balances your portfolio, concentrating in winners of both classes at different speeds.

There is another rule I've found super helpful once you've reached the starter level of your number of stocks you'll buy before adding to existing positions, whether that be 20 -25 or 50 or more, whatever you choose. The rule I still follow today, I can only buy new stocks from my watchlist if none of my current Growth or Value stocks fit my predetermined re-buy criteria outlined above in the examples, i.e., Value +20%, Growth +50%.

This rule can be very hard to stick to when I'm so excited about so many companies on my watchlist! But if you are loath to add to an existing position that has performed well and fits your rebuy minimum criteria, you should reconsider why you hold it in the first place. Remember, ultimately only a relatively concentrated portfolio stands a chance of outperforming the market. If you never want to buy a second share of an existing company you hold, you may as well just buy an index. As your portfolio grows in sheer number of stocks you own, FOMO of other companies you hear about but don't own will subside, and your winners will start to materialize over time. You will stop caring as much about which stocks are winning for other investors and be happy with your own likely surprising mix of winners.

The Takeaways: Determining your own rebuy minimums for Growth and Value stocks makes Stock Planting ™ a workable system for everyone. You don't have to be a stock picking genius, but you do want to determine at what levels you start buying more shares in company stocks you already own. Making these decisions ahead of time frees you from paralysis by analysis that affects many investors. Remain neutral and let your winners sift themselves out from the pack to be re-bought over time, you'll probably be surprised at the odd mix of winners you have.

How to Add to Existing Positions

You just got paid, the automatic monthly deposit has hit your investment account. You have a few stocks that have reached their minimum rebuy percentages and held at or above those levels for a couple of weeks. Remember from our example this minimum rebuy level would be +15% gain for Value stocks, +30% Growth. Or +20% Value, +50% Growth. The question now is how do you know which stock to re-buy first? As to the order, you could add to the company that got above its minimum rebuy level first and maintained above that percentage for the whole waiting period, or you could add to the company that got highest above its rebuy minimum, the choice is yours. Go with the business that excites you most for its future long-term prospects. It could be a company you have previously re-bought, or it could be only a seed position and you're concentrating into it for the first time. I have made varying judgement calls when multiple stocks reach above their rebuy minimums at the same time, it is a great problem to have.

I like this waiting period of 2-4 weeks before I rebuy stocks that have grown past their rebuy minimum percentage. I think of it as a cooling off period, it helps me be neutral to keep things systematized and to take some of the emotion out of the decision. I also make sure that none of the stocks dipped below their respective value or growth rebuy zones at the end of that 2–4-week period, those would have to wait until they re-grew above my minimum levels.

So, the stocks that maintained that elevated level above the rebuy minimum percentage are likely next in line. I have now determined which stock that is, company with ticker XYZ. Now how do I know how many shares to add? Unless you're doing partial or fractional shares, which I will explain momentarily, your stocks have a wide variety of prices among them.

If you add a single share to one of the highest priced stocks in your portfolio, it will make that position an even larger share of the whole account. If you add only a single share to one of your smallest share-priced companies, your portfolio appreciation will be hardly noticeable, even if this company goes on to keep rising in price. I made this latter mistake early on due to being timid and not wanting to commit to having a large (to me) stake in any one company due to fear of loss.

Looking back, I was adding teacups to mountain lakes by buying a single second share of an especially small company in my portfolio that had performed well and reached its rebuy minimum. It's great performance just didn't move the needle in changing my whole account performance, even with a second share. On the other end of the spectrum, when I got overly excited and added multiple shares to higher-priced companies, I was risking early over-concentration by adding to companies that had not earned that high percent stake in my portfolio by merit, but almost by default, due to share price.

As you can probably tell, the early days of my portfolio were a wild west, with a lot of jumping around, buying and selling, without any clear reason or system to any of it. This is why an allocation system like Stock Planting ^{TM} is so necessary, and why I focus on the percentage that the company stock makes up of the entire account; it levels the playing field over time between your higher and lower priced companies.

So, when you are ready to add to the winning stock you've selected, there should be a portfolio tab on your account that lets you see what percentage of the total account each company stock makes up. If not, you can always do this manually by dividing the dollar amount of your current seed share by the total dollar amount of your portfolio. You need to figure out what your target percentage is for any company you're adding to. This could be 2%,3%, 5%, even 10% of the whole account, or whatever figure you come up with. If you have multiple investing accounts, the percent will likely be different, based on the varying total dollar amounts in the accounts. We'll call this ideal target your Stock Nurturing Ratio. Remember that everyone starts in different places, has different risk tolerances and timelines, and has a unique mix and number of stocks, so the first ideal target percentage of the account will be different for everyone.

Another way to think about this concept is to target a percentage that can fall within the top 10 holdings of your account after you re-purchase more shares of your stock that has gone up. Play around with some numbers ahead of time to determine your ideal Stock Nurturing Ratio. Keep in mind this initial ratio percent may have to change, likely be reduced, as your portfolio grows in total dollar size over the years, which is a good thing!

Let's use the example of 5% as a Stock Nurturing Ratio example so we can follow this through. You take your total account balance and multiply it by 0.05. If you had $10,000 in your investment account that day, that would mean your target position after the repurchase would be $500, or 5% of $10,000. If the stock you are adding to had grown to a price per share of $50, and you had saved up at least $450 in your investment account in cash, you would buy 9 new shares of that stock, bringing you up to the 5% target and a total of 10 shares of this company. The total percent growth on the individual stock will fall back out of your rebuy zone into a low positive return, which is a good thing.

Even though some may point out that you are diluting your total return by buying more shares, which is true, winners have a habit of continuing to win, and you may be adding to that stock again before you know it. In addition, since you started with such a small seed, either a single share or a fractional share, leaving that small amount to grow even hundreds of percents won't be as powerful as concentrating more into that position and letting more shares grow.

Following our previous example, if the share price was $60

and not $50, I would buy 8 shares, putting me over that 5% target at $540, as opposed to under the 5% target with 7 shares, leaving me with $480 and 4.8% concentrated in that position. If I did not have the $540 in cash in my portfolio, I would wait until next month's or even the month after's cash deposit, if necessary, before purchasing.

Using this painstakingly patient approach was a hard conclusion for me to come to over the years. I wanted to have enough cash to actually add up to my target percentage (Stock Nurturing Ratio) when I repurchased shares. I felt like I was missing out, (some of that FOMO crept back), and part of me wanted to add one share this month, and the second the next. This is a great rebuying system called dollar cost averaging where you purchase shares of the same investment each week or month to capture both high and low prices of investments. I like to use this elsewhere in my portfolio like my 401(k) plan with mutual funds, but it wasn't what I wanted to do with my single stocks. Everyone's portfolio and system are unique to them, so you can of course do as you'd like. I told myself I'm investing for the long run, hopefully my entire life, so waiting one more month to buy more of that company I liked wouldn't be the end of the world, and would give me the full concentrated position I wanted.

To return to that previous example, if buying a single share of one of my larger companies would put me over the 5% target allocation, I would buy just a single second share. This will happen mostly to you early on, while your portfolio has a small total balance. Some of these questions make it easier in a way to use a brokerage account that lets you use fractional shares. Especially with larger holdings, you can be much more exact in your reallocation targets, getting exactly to that 3 or 5%, or whatever your first Stock Nurturing Ratio target percentage is. You can just enter the total dollar amount you want to buy, and the platform will buy the corresponding amount of shares. If I had to do Stock Planting ™ over again from scratch, I would have likely utilized a brokerage company from the start that let me use fractional shares, for this simplicity.

Inevitably there are 2 follow-up questions that come to mind after implementing this part of the Nurturing Phase; when do I add again to my positions that I just added to, and what do I do if the stocks fall? To answer the first question, as I said previously, adding more shares will dilute the total percent gain for the stock. This sounds like a bad thing, until we remember that you are only starting out with seeds, or very small portions of your portfolio. You will have many stocks that end up poor investments, many that are okay, and a few that are exceptional.

You will be adding to the exceptional stocks. When you add to them, the total return for that holding will drop. The exact amount of the drop will vary with each stock, as it depends on the percentage level it rose to before you added, and how many shares of the company you had to purchase to get to your Stock Nurture Ratio target percentage. The cool part about this is now you don't have to think too much about this company or its stock for a while. If it continues to grow over the coming months and years, now that it is a larger percent of your portfolio, you are taking advantage of that concentration, and the shares rising will be a more meaningful upward lift to your portfolio. You will wait until it passes your minimum rebuy criteria once again and can choose how much additional percent of your portfolio you want that stock to become and buy more shares. It could be the same percentage as the first round, or more, or less, it is up to you, we'll revisit this a bit later. We need to discuss the other side though, what happens if the stock drops right after I concentrate and add to an existing position?

The Takeaways: So far there are two separate sets of percentage figures you need to keep track of to implement this system well. Luckily it isn't that complicated once you get the hang of it. The first is at what positive percent return you will add more shares to a stock, whether it be Growth, or Value.

These were given as examples of Value, +20%, Growth, +50%. The second percentage does not distinguish by Growth or Value, it is your Stock Nurturing Ratio. This percentage is the end goal percent of your total account you want your original share plus your new shares in the company to become. These were given as examples of 3% or 5% of your total account. You've got this!

What Happens If I Add to Stocks that Drop?

This exact drop right after a re-purchase has happened to me, and while it isn't fun, there are a couple of ways I want you to think about these positions that can help alleviate the sting. If the company is a Value stock, it is a dividend paying company. Even with a depressed price, it will continue providing you quarterly or annual dividends of cash deposits into your account. As a sidebar, I don't like reinvesting dividends in the company that provides the dividend. I like letting that cash accumulate to buy more shares of the companies that have risen to their rebuy minimum level, so your dividends aren't adding to losing stocks.

If there are no companies above your rebuy minimums, the dividends will add cash to your cash portion of the account, along with the monthly deposits for your next purchases on your watchlist. At first, the dividends will feel quite meaningless, literally pennies per quarter or year, especially if you do fractional shares. But as you concentrate your winners that do pay a dividend and add more dividend paying companies over time (I love a mix of Value and Growth companies), the dividends can become a more meaningful addition each year to your buying power. I have a couple of awesome dividend-specific strategies that I'll share with you later in the book.

The dividend paying Value companies that have their total percent gain drop right after you buy more shares of them will likely continue to pay this dividend for many years. They are typically but not always slower to rise, and slower to drop. Your Growth stocks will typically but not always be quicker to rise, and quicker to drop. If it is a Growth company that dropped right after you re-bought, don't despair. Although the growth stocks that you've added to are in a concentrated position and don't pay a dividend, remember that they are likely to rise more quickly than Value stocks on good individual company news and/or good industry news, or even overall positive market news and sentiment.

Zooming out to see the bigger picture can be very helpful with stocks that have dropped for you, whether you have one share or many. One of two things will happen with both types - Growth and Value stocks - that have dropped. Either they will rise back into your minimum rebuy level, and you will concentrate additionally into that company, or eventually you will reach the end of your hopefully long holding period and you may decide to sell them, if they never recovered. More on how to think about the holding period later, it is very important to this whole investment process.

The Takeaways: Some stocks continue to rise after you re-buy more shares, others take short or extended drops. You can stop worrying about them either way. They will come back or they will not, you can't control the stocks, but you can reign in your emotions and mentally move on for the time being. The stocks that continue to grow will become a larger and larger part of your account, fueling total account growth along the way up, and those that continue to shrink will become a smaller part of your account, minimizing further account decline as you add new funds monthly and only add to winners.

Contribution Cutoff

The last points I want to discuss in the Nurturing Phase are the need to determine how much to add to companies that you have already previously added to and have risen again to your rebuy minimum (for example Value, +20%, Growth, +50%). The other point is when to stop adding to positions. What has been consistent throughout the book has been my request to focus on the percentages of your account, and not the dollar amounts, and that is no different here.

Returning to our example above, if your first repurchase of a stock was to give it a 3% total account allocation, for the second phase, you may decide on an additional 3% of the total account for 6% total, or whatever additional amount you want to add. Since the stock has appreciated since you bought it, as an example, if you concentrated the stock to be 3% with the first rebuy, then it rose again to above your rebuy minimum, it may already be at 4 or 5% of your total portfolio, depending on how long it took to get there growing as you added cash monthly to the portfolio.

With this second rebuy rule, you can either make a set percentage ahead of time for both types or come up with slightly different percentages if you want for each position or each type, Growth vs Value; the point is to feel comfortable with the ending allocation amount. It may be the first time a single stock position reaches 5% or 10%+ of your account, and it can feel a little unnerving to be that much "in" with one single company. Your brain inevitably starts to visualize what could happen to your portfolio if that stock were to take a large drop. Re-familiarize yourself with the business, and remind yourself why you chose it as a company that could succeed, this often helps calm nerves. Determine what feels best to you and go with that percentage as your second rebuy percent of your whole account. The same would apply for a third or fourth rebuy, if applicable.

The last point we need to discuss in the Nurturing Phase

is incredibly important. This is your Contribution Cutoff, or at what point you stop adding to a single position. This percentage will be different for each investor but is very important to determine ahead of time. Once you reach this, you will no longer purchase additional shares in that company. At the end of the book, I will write down a couple example portfolio's "rules" in a clear format to help it all come together, this cutoff should be a figure you include in yours.

As much as you love companies that have grown in stock price for you over time and helped your portfolio chug along to great heights, determining a stopping point for contributions to any single position can help keep you rational and grounded in what may feel like a very emotional - almost euphoric - positive experience. It can help prevent you from falling into the strange bias that a beloved stock that has performed well for you for years will never let you down (sad hint, some do, and in drastic ways). How do we avoid falling into this? By determining ahead of time, a point at which you'll stop contributing to any single position, and later in the book a point at which you'll start selling.

Let's pretend your Contribution Cutoff is 12%. This means once a stock reaches 11.9% of the account, I would stop buying new shares of that company. To determine this number, I always like to use the litmus test that goes like this: How would I feel if this position was suddenly cut in half? By choosing 12% as my Stock Contribution Cutoff, I am saying that I am "okay" with this 12% position suddenly dropping to 6%. This sizeable 50% drop in share price may sound crazy but does happen with investing in single stocks, even quality companies can be sold heavily in bear markets or due to other singular, unanticipated events within or outside of the company.

Here is a bigger picture way to think about this: if 12% of your portfolio was suddenly cut in half, your whole account would only be down 6%, roughly speaking. If that seems high to you, maybe 12% is too high. If you are younger, have a much longer time until you need the funds for income, or feel like you have a tolerance for risk that is higher and a 6% whole account drawdown doesn't seem so bad, maybe 12% is too low for your Contribution Cutoff. Maybe your contribution cutoff number for a single stock is 15% (that would be a 7.5% portfolio drawdown in a 50% drop), 20% (10% drawdown) or even higher.

I do have to note here that I have observed many people think they are risk-on and overestimate their risk tolerance until a big drawdown slaps them in the face. Then they turn emotional, scared of the future, and panic-sell. Other people are good at holding on but hold too high a percent of their net worth in a single position for too long. After the big drawdown does happen and a sizeable portion of their unrealized net worth with it, they carry regret and anger for years about not trimming back earlier, as if they should have been able to predict the nearly unpredictable market moves. So, this Contribution Cutoff number may change over time, as you get to know yourself as an investor. One of my favorite non-investing books around this topic that has helped me so much with investing is Ryan Holiday's *Ego is the Enemy*. I consider it a must-read for those wanting to learn through stories of history and philosophy how tempering our ego and not telling ourselves untrue narratives can help ground us in so many aspects of our lives, including investing.

The Takeaways: Determine ahead of time at what point (% of the whole account) you'd feel comfortable to stop adding to an existing position. The best of us can be blinded by excess optimism and greed, set your comfort level ahead of time by imagining the stock dropping 50%. What would that do to your account total, and how would that make you feel? Set your Contribution Cutoff for all single positions and try to stick with it, no matter how much you love the company.

Let it Ride

Once you determine your Contribution Cutoff where you'll stop adding to positions, and once one of your positions reaches that point and continues upward, you would not add any new shares to that position, you would Let it Ride. This is a range between your Contribution Cutoff and when you would start trimming the stock. During the Let it Ride phase you will take no action. If in the future the stock falls well below your Stock Contribution Cutoff, you could add it back into the stocks that could be repurchased, if you'd like. If you want to wait for a bit and see how the company and stock do before adding more shares, that is an alright option too.

For those that have been disagreeing about diluting your gains by adding more shares to stocks that have appreciated, this Let it Ride step should help you relax, since at this point you let your winners compound without additional buying. One thing to think about too, is that this is an accumulation strategy, which means you're hopefully able to add new funds to your account each month. These new funds coming in as cash will reduce all the stock holdings' percent of the whole account, and allow you to add to great, winning stocks over longer periods of time.

A stock will really have to outperform to reach the Contribution Cutoff, which is precisely the point; we want to let the winners win, and to have added to them on the way up, taking advantage of the continued compounding growth with more shares of the stock, with each rebuy. If you invest in dozens of stocks, some will likely be terrible, many mediocre, a few great, and one or two could be fantastic market outperformers over the long run, carrying your whole portfolio to some amazing heights. If you invest in hundreds of stocks, curiously the ratios seem about the same, at least that's been my experience. Some terrible, many mediocre, a few great, and fewer still absolutely amazing. Investors love to brag about the few massive hits they got right, no one likes admitting just how many losers they usually had to sift through and lose money on to get those ridiculous outperformers that make headlines.

What you can have is the humbling expectation that even among dozens or hundreds of great companies, we really have little to no idea which will be the star outperformers in the future, especially over the short run, there are just too many factors out of our control. But over the long run, the longer the better, by starting with many small seeds of great companies we're tilting the odds in our favor of buying, holding, and repeatedly adding to one or more of those shooting stars.

The Takeaways: Let it Ride is the "hold" part of buy and hold. In the gap between your Contribution Cutoff and when you start to trim the position, all the empty space in between is for you to sit still and do nothing, and for the stock to do its thing. It will grow slowly or quickly with market and company stock fluctuations, it's never in a straight line. Take pride in your winners, but don't be ashamed of your losers, it is all part of the process.

CHAPTER 10: PHASE 4 - THE TRIMMING PHASE

Take Some Gain

Like many plants and trees that need to be pruned or have some branches trimmed back in various seasons to improve the overall health of the organism, there are two different ways to trim your portfolio that need to be discussed. The first kind of trimming is when a position has reached (to you) a significant percentage of your overall portfolio. At some point, for most investors, you do need to take some gains off the table (finally, some of you say!). I can't stress enough the importance of figuring out this top trimming percentage of your account ahead of time. If you don't determine this in advance, you will be tempted to let the winner ride to an even higher level in your portfolio, not realizing the amount of risk you may be inadvertently taking on.

Everyone has different risk tolerances, but sometimes investors will apply an irrational and emotional level of belief to the idea that because a stock has risen for them for years or even decades, it will continue to rise indefinitely. For some it's a near religious zeal in their belief in the company's future performance based on its products. For others it's the dominant historical stock price performance (up to this point). It could also be old-fashioned greed about how much more money you think you could make by continuing to hold on to an outsized position in your portfolio. Some people hold on to winners far too long in many cases, never curbing risk or taking money off the table.

This may sound contrary to the "let it ride" mentality ascribed just earlier in the book with determining your Contribution Cutoff. However, reallocating in this way not only lets you take some of the profits from your outperformers but reduces your portfolio risk as well. What is the point of investing? For most people, after a long enough time horizon, the answer is to provide future income. Everyone's risk tolerance and needs or wants for investing can be very different. On one end I have heard people terrified of investing in anything outside of cash and CDs (Certificate of Deposits) who are petrified of losing money. All the way to the opposite extreme other people go "all-in" on an early stock, and happen to get very lucky and it becomes a massive percent of their total net worth.

The stories that make me wince the most are those who were lucky and maybe savvy enough to get these early single stock massive, concentrated wins. I am happy that they accumulated an incredible amount of wealth, I genuinely want everyone to win with money, but some never realize (aka take home) any of that wealth, and don't sell anything at all despite certain holdings growing to very outsized portions of their net worth.

These stories are painful because of the end of the story. A year or two later, I hear that some of these individuals were able to build substantial unrealized wealth, even to the point of saying the position had grown enough to pay off their house or retire decades early and more if they were to sell. Yet they are obstinate in not selling because of their belief in the concentrated winner, and when the prices crash later, they are not able to participate in any of the realized gains that could have potentially changed their financial lives. They held on to too much, for too long, relative to the rest of their portfolio. I am not saying they should have sold the entire position, but not taking at least some gains off the table during extended times of extreme portfolio runup has its risks too.

Paper or unrealized gains are something that make you feel good and smart, and even something some would brag to their friends about. But realized gains are the real wealth you actually get to keep once you sell, after taxes, if applicable. These are lucky or savvy investors, and I celebrate their success, but I wish they had taken even a portion of their gains off the table along the way. It is probably not entirely their fault, they likely didn't have a system set up ahead of time like a trimming point, which is what I'm trying to help you do now in case you're ever in a similar situation.

I want to help you realize there is always a chance of large loss by investing in single stocks, no matter how great the company is and how great it may have performed for you up until this point. You can insulate your portfolio against yourself by determining a point where you will start selling shares of your biggest winners. Let's use the example of 20% as someone's selling or Stock Trimming point. I am sure some will have their trimming point be much higher, others lower, it really is dependent upon each person and their perceived risk tolerance, and situation.

In this example of a 20% Trimming point, the investor has determined that 20% is the highest they are comfortable any single position getting to within their portfolio. If the position suddenly declined 50%, the 10% loss to their portfolio is the maximum they would feel "comfortable" sustaining. Nobody wants to lose money, but working through comfortable loss levels in your situation will be helpful in determining your Trimming Point. We know most companies don't decline that fast, but some do, and some decline much more than 50%, all the way down to 90%+ losses very quickly. I have found this mental exercise of a 50% drop a useful rule of thumb when determining my own Stock Trimming point, it is a similar litmus test to determining your maximum Contribution Cutoff in the previous chapter.

Going back to the 20% Stock Trimming example, this individual would start to sell shares once this stock reached 20.1% of their account. They have enjoyed the stock appreciation in this company and want to take some gains off the table. Some might want to sell all their shares at a certain peak percentage, but the downside in selling the entire position could be that they sit out any continued future growth this stock could provide.

The exact way you trim your stocks will also be unique to each investor; you could sell a percentage of the position, say 1% or 2% or even more, or, if the stock price is high enough relative to your portfolio, you could sell a single share at a time, it is up to you. This will reduce your risk down to your trimming point. It will allow you to sell a stock at an appreciable gain and let you continue to hold a good portion of the stock for future growth. You don't have to stress about the position becoming an outsized position in your account, because if it continues to do well, you will simply continue to shave off the top to get it in line with your comfort level. It will also free up some cash for either another stock that is above its rebuy minimum, create some spending money, or free up cash for the next purchase on your watchlist.

Your remaining stock will now likely be in the "Let it Ride" phase, in between your Contribution Cutoff, and your Trimming Point. This is exactly where we want it. As you continue to add cash to your account each month, and the stock price fluctuates, if it continues to grow and outperform and gets back up to this portfolio's example of 20.1%, you will again sell another percent or share, to continue to trim the stock to keep it under your comfortable maximum allocation. If the stock falls, and continues to fall back under your Contribution Cutoff, it may be within your rebuy minimum. It would be your choice whether to let it ride a while longer, or begin adding to it again, until it grows back to your Contribution Cutoff.

The Takeaways: There is always the chance of large losses in single stock investing, prepare accordingly ahead of time. Determine what percentage you want your top holdings to make up within your account. Determine this by imagining the top holdings being suddenly cut in half by percentage, and how you would feel relative to how much of your account that loss would be, in dollars. Once you reach that top percent, start selling either a share or percent at a time, at your comfort level, to keep the top stocks under that maximum. This top percentage will be different for everyone.

Stock Holding Period

The second reason to trim a portfolio (sell some stocks) is when you reach the end of your holding period. Before you buy a single share, while still in your watchlist phase, there are two helpful figures you could come up with ahead of time that will free you up emotionally later when you encounter them.

The first figure to come up with is the holding period for your stocks. We have talked at length about being a long-term investor, and I hope you give your stocks a chance to prove themselves, even if they have been beaten down in the short or medium term. I have heard recommendations for holding periods of one year, three years, and five years. I have even heard holding periods of ten years, or longer. As crazy as it may sound, especially in what has become a bit of an instant-gratification culture, I prefer 10+ years the most. There have been two books that I consider must-reads written about stocks that have gone up 100 times in value. Yes, you heard that right, 100x. The first, an older book called *100 to 1 in the Stock Market* by Thomas William Phelps, and a follow-up to this work in more modern times called *100 Baggers* by Christopher Mayer. I love both books, and I would recommend you read them in historical order (first Phelps' book followed by Mayer's). While they are both full of fantastic anecdotes and historical data, there was one story that really stuck out from 100 baggers.

I'm paraphrasing, but there is a story from back in the day when people bought physical paper shares of stock. A man bought a number of shares in several companies. He was not an investor that tracked the market daily, yearly, or at all really. He put the shares in his safe and did not sell or change anything about them for over ten years. When he passed away about ten years later, his wife brought the shares to their broker, and they were astonished by the results. Some of the shares were worth very little or zero as the companies went out of business or the business stagnated. A few had done okay, somewhat above and below keeping up with the general market returns of the previous 10 years. A single company's stock gain had powered incredible market-crushing gains, lifting the entire portfolio including the duds, well above the market return for those 10 years. Sound familiar?

This longer period of inactivity and a little bit of luck in choosing the one out of dozens that did so well, made up for the losses or market underperformance in all the other stocks, and that position had gone up 100 times in value. The long-term, mostly boring journey most 100x investments take requires incredible investor patience waiting through different market cycles.

Many times, these stocks had been available for years at prices that would then go up 100x in value, so you're not always missing out or too late, as it is easy to believe with FOMO. Phelps said investors must have the skill to find the stocks, the courage to buy them, and the patience to hold them. Another of my favorite quotes from his book, "In Alice and Wonderland, one had to run fast to stand still. In the stock market, the evidence suggests that one who buys right must stand still, in order to run fast." So, while each of you will need to determine how long you want to hold stocks before you sell losers, I hope you look to the longer tail of that range, 5-10+ years as a consideration.

I would encourage you to pull up Yahoo finance or Google finance or whichever tracker you like and pull up several companies' stock performance. Look at the maximum return period. For companies older than 10, 20, or even 50-100 years, it can be very enlightening to see that despite many ups and downs along the way, many, but not all, simply took a long time to figure out their business in a way that the market eventually rewarded dramatically. I am not advocating to only buy older companies' stock, I like a good mix of old and new, but it helps zooming out to see that you would have had many chances to purchase great winners along the way, many years after they initially went public, and with certain winners still compounded incredibly above the average stock market return.

To see how this holding period works in practice, here is an example. Let's say you've determined your holding period is 8 years. At the end of those 8 years for a stock you purchased, you would first look back at the performance of the stock over that time, comparing that with a benchmark index like the S&P 500, (the US top 500 companies by size, grouped together in one index) for the same time period. You could also compare the company's return for those 8 years against others in its field, but I do like the benchmark index performance, to determine if you had been better off just buying the index than that particular stock. Eight-ten years is likely a long enough time to measure that I believe if a company had a secret sauce of intrinsic value or outperformance of earnings or something else, you should have started to see some of that manifest in the stock price. If you were unlucky enough to buy your seed share at the absolute peak before a large market crash, as may happen, additional consideration would need to be given. This is why measuring against a benchmark is so useful to see what the rest of the market was doing during that time.

Let's first imagine your stock has underperformed the benchmark by a wide margin. Some companies will take longer than your holding period to have the good business performance match the price movement of the stock, or it may never achieve that market value you think it "deserves". Investors and the market are not always rational, as we know.

Try to be objective in looking through the company's financial situation over your holding period, whether it improved or worsened, whether any new products, services, or acquisitions may have improved or worsened your outlook on the company. Look to whether leadership changes, if any, had a positive or negative impact on your view of the company. Looking forward, do you believe over the next 8-10 years it can turn around and outperform, or continue to underperform?

Act as if you've never bought the stock, and to use a sunk-cost analysis, each day you continue to hold, you are in essence committing to re-buy it each day. If the stock and more importantly the company doesn't still make you excited being an investor, it may be time to sell. Try to look at your original thesis for investing, and take any lessons learned as to what went wrong either with the business or your criteria for a good investment, so you can apply it to future watchlist ideas.

Now, if the stock has roughly kept up with the market, and you go through the same exercises above, if you're still excited about it, you may want to keep holding for an additional holding period (8 years in our example). Or, if you see clouds on the horizon after doing some research and think the company may be running out steam, it may be time to sell, it is all up to you. Remember though that negative news is easier to sell than positive, and that is no exception for company forecasts. There will likely be many reasons to sell, with fewer reasons to buy, for most stocks, at most times.

For stocks that have outperformed the market over your holding period, if you are uneasy that their best days may be behind them due to some changes in the company or industry that the company is in, you may want to sell some or all of the shares. I like the idea of selling a portion instead of the whole position if you feel the need to sell, because as we have mentioned many winners keep on winning despite our short-term gloomy analysis! If the stock has outperformed the market, and you're as excited and confident as ever in the business' ability to keep succeeding, then you may not want to sell any shares, but keep holding for an additional 8-10 years, or whatever your holding period is, and repeat the process.

Here is the last mental exercise that I like to walk through when analyzing a company at the end of my holding period.

If you had to recommend this stock to a dear friend or family member, especially one new to the market and investing, why would you recommend it? Why might you avoid it? If you can't come up with compelling reasons other than the historical stock price appreciation, it may be time to rethink holding it, or at least to consider trimming part of your position.

The Takeaways: Utilizing a longer holding period for the quality stocks you buy can help you not worry if the stock performance lags in the short or medium term. It runs against our nature to hold stocks for long time periods as we are naturally fearful of the future unknown and of losing money, but the long holding periods are what give us a chance to outperform. With time and patience being invested in the markets, the fear and knee-jerk sell reactions subside. Remember, "one who buys right must stand still, in order to run fast".

Trim Losing Stocks

Unfortunately, the sad fact is that some stocks never come back to levels previously reached (aka the price you bought them) while they are within your holding period. A reason to sell a stock might be that the stock has reached a specific total percentage loss. You might want to cut your loss and not wait 2 or 5 more years (or however long until the end of your holding period) before selling. Figuring out a maximum sell percentage ahead of time can help you be neutral about the situation when it happens to you.

You have learned your lesson, researched what may have gone wrong with the company to have such a drastic downturn, and can move on and allocate those dollars to hopefully future winners. I hope this selling point is a high percentage number. That is, I hope you don't sell after a -20% or even -40% loss, as crazy as that may sound to some readers. I have seen some companies' stock recover from lower levels than that and sail back into positive territory once the company fixes what needed fixed with the business and positive momentum kicks in. This doesn't happen overnight, it usually takes a few years, but it can happen. To immediately counter myself, some stocks never do recover from those lows, so this selling point will be a personal preference, like everything else in running your Stock Planting ™ portfolio.

Of course, each person will need to come up with their own cutoff percentage, but let's pretend yours were as an example -70% total loss. Once a stock reached that low, you could take one final look through reports, earnings calls, articles etc. You are searching for positive reasons to hold it any longer, and if none are found then sell, if that is what feels right for you to do. Move on to adding to existing winners or adding new companies from your watchlist, whichever phase you're at.

Remember from the first part of the book that no one is watching or cares about the losers in your portfolio except you;

no one is hounding you quarter to quarter or year to year to improve your returns, especially in single positions. This anonymity can give you peace and patience over your losing stocks, instead of hurt pride and anger at yourself or the company. What if you did sell, what would have to change to compel you to re-buy the stock later? A business change or stock price change? Statistically you likely never will re-buy it; you're too emotionally stung from the large loss. Thinking through some of these ideas and how they apply to your temperament can help you determine what your personal maximum sell range is.

Managers often feel they must sell losers quickly, and while the incredible Warren Buffet even ascribes to that philosophy generally, he has admitted to short-term thinking and selling a few positions that cost him later when he sold out too early. Of course, he has performed phenomenally as an investor, but none of us are immune to our own short-term behavior. I don't trust my own short-term thinking, which is why I rely on the systems within Stock Planting ™ to help keep me in check. I have found it hard to determine if my short-term losers really are losers or just oversold by investor pessimism, a series of bad earnings periods, or business fumbles. Luckily, I don't have any shareholders or board members breathing down my neck about losses and am quite patient, so I tend to sell slowly with a very high maximum loss percentage, but it will be to each person's preference, as is this entire system.

To attempt to outperform the market and hopefully have some fun and make money doing so along the way, a longer time horizon of many years seems necessary in almost all cases. The stocks almost never go straight up and to the right, there is so much zigging and zagging, large leaps, and devastating falls. But time is on your side, and the longer your time horizon, the longer you can let good companies and people within those companies innovate and improve, and their stocks can have a chance to provide you incredible returns.

One of my favorite parts of this approach is that the more some of my stocks underperform, the less I have to care about them, because they make up an increasingly tiny portion of my portfolio. If you think about it, a stock that has been beaten down -70 or -80% makes up an insubstantial portion of your account given enough time and new funds being added to your account each month. Whether the stocks down there at the bottom 10% of your portfolio perform well or not in a given day, month, or year doesn't really matter to your portfolio's growth or decline like your top holdings do and is more a passing interest.

There is an easy way to think about this visually on your computer or phone once you're well into your Stock Planting ™ system. Your 25+ stocks have likely segregated roughly into thirds. The bottom ⅓ which are likely -40%+ returns, you can basically ignore. You're aware of them, you'd love for them to make a comeback someday, but since they have become such a small part of your portfolio, any large or small gains or losses on these now tiny positions don't really move the needle at all in your portfolio on a given day or month, or even year. Selling them won't yield you significant cash since they have dropped so much. You may as well hold them to the rest of your holding period since large surprises to the upside happen all the time in the stock market, especially over a few years.

Your middle ⅓ are likely stocks that are roughly between -20% and +5%, and these merit more interest than the bottom ⅓ . But they are not likely stocks you're going to rebuy or sell anytime soon, they will need to prove themselves better and move up into more positive territory to merit rebuy, but you're rooting for them! If you're going to be a successful single stock investor, you must be comfortable with the fact that many stocks will remain in the red for you in different seasons.

The top ⅓ of your portfolio is by far the most exciting and all in the green. You have seen some single stocks appreciate wonderfully. These companies' stock (not often the ones I would have thought would be there) are either:

a) getting close or ready for repurchase soon above your rebuy minimum, or

b) are above your contribution cutoff and in the Let It Ride phase, or

c) are close to your top single position (Trimming point) and will be trimmed back soon if they keep growing at such a great rate.

This is the best part of the process, to see that among some duds, you've picked and added to some great stocks, and are enjoying watching them become a larger part of your portfolio over time as you add to them, increasing the odds for wonderful portfolio returns.

The Takeaways: Try to think about what a maximum acceptable percent loss on a stock looks like for you before you'd sell. Hopefully it's a high loss, you never know what can happen and you're unlikely to re-buy it later if you sell, but this max drawdown will be different for everyone. Your portfolio will naturally segment into rough thirds, with the bottom third becoming more inconsequential over time, the middle third idling, and the top third likely growing like crazy. You'll be surprised which picks end up where, that is part of the (humbling) fun!

How Often Should You Monitor Your Portfolio?

If all of this sounds overwhelming and that there is no way you'll have enough time to manage a portfolio like this with your busy life, I want to walk you through how much or little time you need to monitor and analyze your portfolio. Once you have it set up, it is fairly easy to manage in a given month. Most everyone's life is quite busy with work, family, friends, hobbies, and many great things to take up our time other than staring at our portfolio's slow growth, which is typically about as exciting as watching paint dry.

It will be a bit of work and time building out your watchlist and initial seed positions of 25+ stocks, whatever number you determine is good for you before you start adding to existing positions. The amount of research you do before buying seed positions is completely up to you, an exhausting amount of research into your watchlist won't guarantee better returns. Since you're buying seed positions, don't stress yourself out too much with this, most people are terrible at picking stocks, because no one can predict all the future factors that affect each stock. Once you have figured out your own percentages of when to rebuy (rebuy minimums), what percent to target with your rebuy, when to stop buying winning positions, and when to start trimming those winners, your portfolio likely doesn't need as much ongoing work as you think.

Once you have your portfolio seed positions and your watchlist set up, you could get away with checking in as little as once per week, or if you're incredibly busy, once every 2 weeks, in line with your possible bi-monthly contributions to your investment accounts from your paychecks. If you check in on it infrequently, you may want to note the date each time when any of your positions cross into their respective rebuy minimums, because the next time you log in, you may have several that reached that minimum percent gain while you were away. If that is the case, you could choose to buy the one that has gotten the furthest above the respective Value or Growth rebuy minimum, or the one you are most excited about that is above the minimum.

If you want to be more involved and check on your account daily but only have time for once per day, checking after 4pm ET, after the market has closed, would be the most productive use of that once daily check-in. If you have time to check twice per day, you could check at the market open, any time after 9:30 am ET, for curiosity's sake as to what stocks are moving early on, but not to take any actions.

I really like David Gardner's advice: if you open your computer and see only a sea of red numbers for the daily returns, then the total market is getting punished, and likely your single stock portfolio is getting punished even worse, as single stock price swings are usually more exaggerated up and down from the market indexes. His advice? (Paraphrased) Close the laptop, go outside, and do or think about anything else. Pursue other hobbies, spend time with family or friends. Anything to prevent you from panic selling or getting depressed watching your stocks tumble.

I would add if the stock market has periods of bad weeks, months, even a year or more, scale back your time allotted to viewing your portfolio for your sanity's sake, and spend more time in the real world, with real people, doing real things. It will probably remind you that the world has kept spinning while your portfolio is crashing, and people are still going about their lives. The markets and your accounts will probably recover, sooner or later.

Hopefully you've been able to take the first section of the book and set up your financial foundation situation to where you don't need the money immediately in your investment accounts. You have time and continued contributions on your side. If you've properly steeled yourself and haven't sold your stocks due to the drop, nothing real has happened to your life with your investments value dropping. This is just an emotional adjustment to your perceptions of future spending expectations, being altered. That's all investing is on a personal level, right?

The funny thing is those future expectations may come roaring back much better than you had anticipated before the drop. There are likely periods of extended great stock market performance in store, I just can't predict the future and tell you when. With a long enough view and sticking to your Stock Planting ™ system, over time you can become better at riding these ups and downs with more equanimity.

Mixed market days, I call them Christmas Light days, where red and green seem to alternate like Christmas lights down your list of holdings, are fun to see which of your holdings are doing well amid a flat total market day. And of course, the greatest dopamine hit a single stock investor like us can get are the really great green days, where your single stock portfolio is likely crushing the general market returns for that day. Even for just one day, you feel like a vindicated genius! You ride that high, giving yourself high-fives (because no one else cares), until the next round of red selloff brings you humbly back to earth. What an exciting time it is to be a single stock investor!

I don't recommend constantly checking on your portfolio throughout the day even for those of you who have the time, everything between the market open and close is just noise for long-term investors like us. I think it will take up more mental time and energy than is productive for you. I personally do like checking once per day, usually after the market closes. If I see massive moves either up or down in my positions or top watchlist stocks it can be nice to find out why, but it's curiosity not desperation, thanks to having a system in place I can be neutral.

Unless there is a massive piece of news that fundamentally changes the company or your thesis for investment, the nice thing about a system like Stock Planting ™ is that you don't really have to care about the short-term news. Most of it will sort itself out over time, only one of three outcomes can occur:

1) The company stock will continue to gain and win for you, and you'll continue to buy it over time.
2) It will deteriorate down to your maximum sell limit, and you'll sell.
3) It will be hang out in the middle somewhere, and at the end of your holding period, hopefully 5-10+ years, you'll decide to sell, or continue to hold for another period.

Everything else in the middle is often just noise.

The Takeaways: You can be as active or passive as you'd like in checking in with your stocks on a daily, weekly, or monthly basis. With this system you'll likely only be taking action (buying) once or twice per month or less as your deposits come in, even less frequently once your account grows significantly and you have to save up more for rebuys, so you don't have to stress if you don't have much time to monitor it. You'll have high highs some days checking in, and gloomy days other times checking in, better to quickly exit the screen on those days. For all of us there is more to life than investing. Spending time pursuing hobbies or with friends and family can put things into perspective and remind you the world keeps spinning outside the stock market.

PART III - ALTERNATIVES, Q&A, THE CLOSE

CHAPTER 11: ALTERNATIVE INVESTMENTS TO THE STOCK MARKET

Precious Metals

Precious Metals can be right for some investors but have never appealed to me. While some have touted them as inflation hedges, that is generally only true over extremely extended time periods, such as over a century or more. If you choose to invest in precious metals, there are many options available. Always keep in mind how liquid or illiquid (easily accessible for sale and use) the different ways to purchase the metals are, as well as the possibility of large loss due to theft of a physical holding if you choose to go that route.

Real Estate Investing

For many people, real estate investing beyond their primary residence can be a great way to diversify from the stock market and have potential future cash flow for many years or even decades. These rental properties can be fantastic investments. I know many people who have done well in direct real estate ownership as an investment, and prefer it to the stock market. I believe you should invest in what you are most comfortable with, and for some that will be all real estate, or a mix of stocks and real estate.

However, for many investors, especially those starting out, having the capital (cash) to put a reasonable down payment on an investment property (10-20%+) can be out of reach financially, especially early on in their careers. There are some companies that allow you to invest a much smaller amount in a property or group of properties directly, this can be the right fit for some people. I know everyone is different, and I applaud investing success in any ethical form. For myself, I don't like the idea of becoming a landlord and needing to be available at all hours or having the extra cash on hand to do repairs and maintenance, it is not an area I see myself thriving in. In *Dividend Growth Investing* by Freeman Publications, I love what they say. "Real Estate is not always a passive investment. If a pipe bursts at 3:00 in the morning, you'll need to actively attend to it."

I do not have many handyman type skills, so if I did own investment property I would have to outsource all repairs via property management which would further dilute my earnings. Also, if I saved up enough and purchased an investment property, it would immediately become a massive percent of my total investment portfolio tied up in one investment, high enough to make me uncomfortable. Again, it can be right for the right investor, and I celebrate everyone winning, so if that is you, then great. For myself, since I'm so much more comfortable with the stock market and investing that way, I'll tell you how I invest in real estate outside of my primary residence.

Real Estate Investment Trusts

It is very simple. I opened an additional Roth IRA separate from my Roth IRA that I buy single stocks in. Remember, you can have any number of IRA's open, but between them all (including Roth and Traditional) you can't contribute more than the maximum limit each year, given your age. So, I put a small portion of my monthly investing dollars into this separate Roth IRA, and I only buy publicly traded Real Estate Investment Trusts, REITs for short, in this account. REITs are set up to generate cash. REIT companies must pass through 90% of their taxable income to their shareholders each year in the form of a dividend. REIT companies invest in a variety of commercial, residential, government, corporate, and industrial sectors, and you can find those that specialize in niche sectors, or those that have broad holdings.

There are REIT ETFs you can buy, but I prefer holding the REIT single stocks directly, and getting all of the income and no expense ratio that I would get with a REIT ETF. I follow a very similar system to my Stock Planting ™ system outlined above. I start with a single share of a REIT, and although I have a lower rebuy minimum for REITs than for single stocks, I follow the same program. Once a REIT grows to that rebuy minimum percent, I purchase more shares to get it to my first level of concentration within the account.

Similar to my stock accounts, I don't reinvest the dividends directly into the company that produced the dividend, I hold the cash for either reinvestment into winning REITs over time, or if no REITs are above my rebuy minimum when I have newly contributed funds come into my account, I purchase a share of the next company on my smaller and separate REIT watchlist, following the 4 phases of Stock Planting ™ laid out in this book.

The beauty of this simple system, and investing via a Roth IRA, is that when I started, the quarterly or monthly dividend payments were literally pennies from the respective shares.

They still aren't very large dividends now, but I know that will change over the decades as my positions grow both in growth and by buying more shares. Passive income is such a buzzword in the financial community, but there is a reason; having your money work for you in a way that provides income indefinitely is such a cool idea.

Each investor who does this REIT investing will likely do it differently, but for me, the reason I chose the Roth IRA for this strategy, is that when I turn 59.5 (or whatever the penalty-free age for withdrawals from retirement accounts is at that time), if I am retired by then, I could adjust how the dividends are paid out. Instead of using the dividends for reinvestment, I could change it so that the brokerage company sends me a monthly check for all dividend income. By that time, I will have been doing my REIT Roth IRA strategy for decades, so that 90% of passthrough income from the REIT companies (which hopefully by then is substantially bigger than the pennies per quarter today), will come out completely tax-free as a passive income stream.

The account would only be able to grow through capital appreciation (growth) at that point but I could partly live off the interest earned for hopefully decades more. Thinking about how different parts of your portfolio will eventually supply you income in retirement is a long-term way to think. As with everything in this book, your personal strategy, percent of your portfolio that is stocks, cash, real estate etc. is unique to you; this is hopefully just a new idea to think about, especially for those who want to invest in real estate but don't have the ability to easily get invested in physical properties.

Investing in REITs in a non-qualified investment account instead of a Traditional or Roth IRA is another way to look at dividend investing outside of retirement accounts. This would require you to pay taxes each year on the dividend income from REITs which can be at a slightly higher rate than normal dividends. You could also use dividend stocks or a combination of REITs and dividend stocks in the same account to diversify your income producers. This could be right for those who don't want to wait until age 59.5 to receive this passive monthly income stream and can access it earlier, and I like this idea a lot as well. These funds and income would be available pre-retirement age, but unlike the Roth IRA, whenever you sell the principal investment if ever, you would have more tax implications to consider. This is another angle to the passive income goal we hear so much about, an idea to get you thinking about working toward the day your investments can pay part or all your monthly bills, granting you financial freedom. If you're interested in learning more about REIT investing, there is a great book I recommend called *REIT Investing for Beginners* by Freeman Publications, which can walk you through many more details of REIT investing.

The takeaways: Direct real estate investing can feel out of reach for many, but there are ways with investment accounts that everyone can participate if they want. Publicly traded REITs can be a great way to generate rental income without having to lift a finger. Although the gains will be minimal and slow at first, over time this could grow to a great passive income stream, whether before or during retirement. Others may prefer the direct ownership route, go with what best fits your situation and personality.

Cryptocurrencies

There are types of investments, typically ETFs, that can add leverage to 2x or even 3x the daily positive and negative returns of an underlying index or stock. These are considered very risky, and most advise not to hold them longer than a day. The reason I bring them up under the Cryptocurrency section, is I believe if there were a product that were able to provide an additional 2x or 3x leverage on one of those ETFs that already have 2x or 3x leverage, that would adequately describe the feeling of investing in cryptocurrencies! The volatility and uncertainty in the space makes it feel like the wild west of investing, new and untamed. Everyone says the cryptocurrency market is not correlated to the stock market, yet there are many days where it seems if the stock market is up, crypto is through the roof, and if the stock market is down, crypto gets punished much worse. This is purely my opinion and limited experience, of course.

I admit I am very ignorant in this new investing world of cryptocurrency, but it has been very helpful in learning to invest in things in which I have no control of the outcomes, but a long-term optimistic view of the investing space. I don't know which projects or specific currencies will end up working out, but I think the long-term outcome of the market will produce some winning stores of value and use cases, I just don't know which currencies and when. This feels similar to single stocks in some ways but with more uncertainty about the project's future, and an underlying business that can be harder to understand for me than single stocks. I only buy tiny fractional shares of cryptocurrency coins. (Cue the ridicule shifting from what was coming from "can't beat the general market with single stocks" guys throughout the book, now coming from crypto guys that are laughing at my timid baby steps into their world - you just can't win!)

Investing even a little bit in crypto has made me a better stock investor by learning to embrace volatility and risk over the short-term (or long term, who knows?). Similar to the real estate section, invest in what you're comfortable with, or what you can slowly become comfortable with over time with more learning and small steps into it. Everyone's path, timeline and investing goals will be different along their investing journey, and that is what is so fun about learning from other people in a variety of investing fields.

The takeaways: If you want to learn more about cryptocurrency there are many great resources out there, including the Bankless podcast and others, and many helpful articles explaining everything and how to get started.

CHAPTER 12: COMMONLY ASKED QUESTIONS

Q: How do I know if Stock Planting TM is for me?

There is a relatively simple exercise I'd like you to do if you're seriously considering adding Stock Planting ™ to your portfolio. Open an investment account with one of the online brokerage companies that permit fractional share purchases. Link this account to your checking account. Fund the account with $50. Research and create a watchlist of 10 stocks. It may take a few days to link your account, and another few days for the cash to be available to buy shares once you've sent it over via ACH, so you have time, no rush. Vary these 10 stocks as much as possible by large and small market cap (company size), Value stocks (dividend paying), and Growth stocks (non-dividend). Include some small new companies, and some old legacy companies. You could even throw in a REIT or an ETF fractional share as well if you'd like, the point is to have a good mix. In picking the companies you could think of competitive advantages, strong brands you like, popular stocks, sleepy stocks with competitive moats or lots of free cash flow, whichever aspects appeal to your investing style. There are many other criteria you could use for your investing thesis of why you think these stocks may perform well in the future. Don't overly stress about the stock selection, it's just $5 per position, and this first step is all for your learning benefit. No one will become rich or impoverished by a $50 investment, so relax.

Once you have your watchlist with your top 10 stocks, purchase a fractional share of $5 of each of the stocks all on the same day during trading hours. Now do nothing. This inactivity may be the hardest part for many new investors. We are naturally wired to want to "do something", yet this exercise is teaching us to do just the opposite. Sit still, go about your life, and observe how the stocks move day to day, week to week, and month to month. Sort your stock list by total percent gain with the highest returning at the top. Now sit still, adding no new funds, for up to 6 months to get comfortable with the system. I predict you'll be surprised which were your 6-month winners, and which stocks your short-term losers. If after 6 months you thought this was a waste of time and not at all interesting, either leave the positions in place or go ahead and cash out if you'd rather. Your account will likely be worth within $45-$55 dollars depending on how your stocks performed, nothing life-changing either way. You can go back to low-cost index funds via mutual funds or ETFs the rest of your life, and still do great, Stock Planting ™ isn't for everyone.

However, if you found the 6-month period (could be only 1-3 months later if you're enjoying it) exciting checking in on your stocks, and you felt the fear of single stock ownership subside as you became comfortable with the fluctuations, then buy another 10 new stocks with another $50. You now have 20 positions, a great start to a Stock Planting ™ journey. As you get increasingly comfortable and your budget permits, you can begin adding more each month to this account and start buying more shares of your winners as they begin to grow above your rebuy minimums, and really begin your Stock Planting ™ experience. You're on your way!

Q: What About Lump Sum Additions to Your Investing Accounts?

I have written the book as if you've just started out investing or have been investing only in your 401(k) plan and want to learn more, but everyone is at different places and ages in their life. I want to address thinking about what you would do if you got an unexpected bonus or inheritance.

If it makes sense with the tax qualification of the windfall (unexpected funds), going back and further shoring up your financial foundation could be a good move for you; it all depends on how you're doing financially when that windfall lands, and what feels best to you at that time of your life. If you are going to allocate some or all of that windfall to investing and in particular single stocks, it is helpful to look at the lump sum through the lens of large ratios.

Look at your current ratios (a portion of your net worth divided by your whole net worth) of cash, real estate (whether physical properties or REITs or both), mutual funds in your 401(k), and single stocks, and any other asset class you own. If investing all of the funds in single stocks would make single stocks too great a percent of your portfolio as to make you uneasy, a few ideas for the cash are: You could pay down some real estate debt if applicable, you could increase your cash position if that made you feel best, or you could buy boring low-cost ETFs or mutual funds in a taxable brokerage account to bring your investment ratios in line with your comfort level. If the inheritance or windfall is with qualified or retirement money, it would have different tax implications, and if that were the case, meeting with a tax expert may make sense.

This same mentality should apply if you have changed jobs and had a 401(k) at your previous job. You can roll this to an IRA or Roth IRA that lines up with the tax qualification of the 401(k) funds if you don't want to keep it managed by the previous 401(k) provider or rolled to your new 401(k) plan at your new job. Due to the fees on 401(k) plans that we've discussed previously, I am in the camp of rolling it away to manage on your own, but everyone's abilities and time to dedicate to investing is different, so it may make sense for some people to leave it where it is. But if you do roll it over, typically the best strategy is to do what is called trustee to trustee, to keep everything behind the tax wall. You don't want to receive the funds yourself, if possible, to avoid an accidental large taxable event. Please speak with a financial advisor to help you on this task if needed, you don't want to get it wrong.

Now let's assume you've figured out the best use for that windfall given its tax status and your life situation, and you still want to invest a good chunk into your single stock account or accounts. I would return to the steps laid out earlier in the book, in most cases I would still only start with opening new positions with a single share. If you have a very high income, or the lump sum is massive, you could start with 10+ shares or a set percent ratio of your account, but those would likely be outlier situations. What is cool about large additions is that it will immediately change the ratios in your account, reducing all of your current holding's percent of the total account by a small or large amount, depending on the size of the addition. You have likely noticed this same phenomenon occurs but on a smaller level each month when the monthly deposit from your paycheck comes into your investing account.

So, stocks that were previously in the "let it ride" stage could likely now be repurchased, bringing them back up to the new account percent balance that you're comfortable with. Or, if you're happy with where those are at and don't want to add to these existing shares, you could simply start adding many stocks that were on your watchlist to now be single share or fractional share seed positions in your account and follow your program on predetermined percentages. It is all up to you, which is the best part. The simplicity of my system is that there is no such thing as too many stocks, or one right way to do it, the ratios are up to you. I want to empower you as an investor to customize your portfolio in the way that makes the most sense to you and where you're at in life.

Q: What if I Work for a Publicly Traded Company?

This can be an amazing, life-changing benefit for some individuals who work at companies whose stock crushes the market during the years they are working for that company and regularly buy or are given large amounts of the company's stock. But for each of those companies, there are also stories of individuals working at companies like Enron or others who went bankrupt. The "loyal" employees who made the company stock contributions an outsized portion of their wealth, saw much of their personal wealth dissipate with the demise of their company and its failing stock. Remember, wealth is what you keep, not what you earn. So, if you do work in one of these companies, treat it the same as if it were your top performing stock in your Stock Planting ™ account described in the Stock Trimming section. Do the litmus test: if the worth of your shares suddenly dropped 50%, how much does that change your life? The answer will be different for everyone, it is a way to think about the stock to personalize it to your situation. Looking at the ratio of what percent of your total net worth is tied up in this one stock including all retirement, investing, and savings accounts is another litmus test of your comfort level with the outsized stock holding.

Q: Should I limit the number of Stocks I own?

I have heard people say that you shouldn't own too many companies' stocks because it is hard to keep up with them, and you need to stay current on news, earnings, or earnings forecasts that may affect the future stock price. All these things likely will affect the future stock price, especially the short-term price, but they are all out of your control. In addition, no one can predict the future, and how different unforeseen events may affect even good companies. I think the above advice about keeping up with all the details of a business would be relevant if you concentrated heavily into just a few stocks, or if your buy and sell determinations were purely fundamental based on financials changing or your perceived threats or advantages to the business. This would also be the case if you were a short-term investor. This is the more typical way to approach a concentrated stock portfolio and is a way some individuals accrue fantastic wealth. Others using the same methodology lose big, betting big on ideas that don't work out, some of which is chalked up to plain old bad luck. You will get portfolio concentration eventually through Stock Planting ^{TM}, but you don't have to go "all-in" initially on just a few companies that may or may not be better than the market, despite much analysis. You can spread your initial risk out by averaging in with much small starter positions.

I don't think any number of stocks is too many, because if you start with a single share or fractional share of a company, this is such a small percentage of your portfolio. You only need to "keep up" with them once they do extremely well or extremely poorly. If you've set up ahead of time a system of parameters of when to re-buy, when to stop buying, when to start trimming, your holding period, and your maximum drawdown of when you'd sell, then you don't have to worry about what you can't control; the performance of the stocks themselves. One of three things will happen to your purchased share:

1. The stock will go up; you will continue to buy it by degrees until your Contribution Cutoff when you Let It Ride until you have to start Trimming it to keep it at your chosen maximum percentage of your portfolio for any one position. This is the best-case scenario and a true winner.

2. It will fall to a maximum drawdown percent return where you decide to sell. This is the worst-case scenario.

3. It will hang out somewhere in the middle, perhaps being re-bought once or twice or not at all, and after that holding period you'll determine either to hold on for another period or sell. This is the most likely of the 3 scenarios.

Stock Planting ^{TM} frees you to focus on other things in your life, allowing you to pull back and check in on your portfolio once per day, week, or even month, at your interest level. It can remove much of the stress of thinking about how the economy or overall market sentiment will affect your stocks. In bull markets you will likely be rebuying more positions you already own, and can be excited about getting more concentration in companies that have proven themselves winners in your portfolio. In bear markets you may have no stocks to rebuy, so you'll be opening many new starter seed positions in new companies from your watchlist, and you can be excited about that! I have found that in both bear and bull markets, it is never quite so black and white; some companies perform well in a bear market and others get crushed in a bull market. Most of all, I am constantly surprised at which companies continually outperform, and which other companies I never rebuy a second share due to terrible performance, that had once seemed so promising when I bought my first share.

Like most of us, I am terrible at predicting the short and medium-term future movements of the stock market, let alone any one company's future stock performance. But I have learned to be great at adapting over time as the winners and losers reveal themselves. If you own a few dozen, hundreds or even over a thousand stocks in your portfolio over the decades, it can be the right fit for you if you've determined your approach and are committed to it. One of the hardest aspects of Stock Planting ™ is the great deal of patience required, especially watching companies you were excited about slip and wallow in low share prices for years. Some will only be seed positions, others will be companies you have rebought earlier, those sting worse. Taking a stoic view is necessary for success with this system. Some stocks come back spectacularly, others not at all, but with too short a holding period, you guarantee that you won't get access to those late bloomers.

Q: What is the Right Price to Buy Stocks?

Of course, if you pay less for a stock, your starting point will be lower, duh. If that stock goes on to great heights, your total return will be higher than if you started with a higher price. The problem is it can be hard to know what the "right" price is to enter. One of my favorite investing quotes by David Gardner is "dips wait for dips". Many wait on the sidelines for months or years, thinking a company's stock price is "overvalued", and wait for a low point to enter. To the frustration of that reluctant investor the "overvalued" company's stock may continue to go up for years, getting further and further away from the investor's arbitrary perfect entry point. It is simply very hard to know. Buy stocks regularly when you have the cash in your investment account, timing the market is very hard to do. Some will turn out later to be great entry points, others not quite as great.

This is why the Seed approach, investing very little at first, either a single share or a fractional share, allows you to have a point of reference on when to rebuy and commit more of your investing dollars to that company. If you were lucky enough to buy the position at a low price that then takes off, you may be re-buying it soon. With others, if you were unlucky enough to buy at a peak followed by a large decline, then yes, at least in the short term, you certainly overpaid. However, since you invested only a small portion of your investment dollars in that position, it will become a less and less significant percent of your overall account over time as you add cash monthly to your account and add to other positions that are performing well over time.

You bought that short-term losing position because you had a thesis on why it may be a great company to own for the future. Since hopefully you have a long holding period, 5-10 years before you sell unless it goes to your lowest cutoff point, you are giving the company and the stock time to recover. Time to adapt to the shifting economy, management, industry, or whatever issues caused the price to drop after you purchased it. With enough time and some luck, the company's stock may recover all the way back into positive territory for you, proving itself a good buy after all, just one you had to wait for. Or it may not recover, in which case you're glad you only had the one share of that losing stock, as you added to other winners instead.

If you're a very high-income earner and the single share idea drives you crazy since it's such a tiny portion of your investing dollars each month, you could up that to a percent of your account as a starting base, or 10+ shares, it is your system. But for most investors new to single stock investing and with normal incomes, I still like the single share or fractional share method best. Most people are blown away by just how volatile single stocks can be, and the single share and fractional share approaches give you time and temperament to get used to the new investing environment without risking a large portion of your hard-earned money. The right time to buy stocks is when you have the money in your account. Thanks to Stock Planting ™ I always have a game plan for the day of the month my deposits hit my account, and just buy shares that day. Some days seem like I'm buying into single day gains, other days like I'm buying into single day losses. What's funny is that by the end of the day, the market has even sometimes flipped, so I end up with the opposite result, which is why I don't really try to time it. Single day returns are mildly interesting, but aren't going to change my financial life, whether with seed positions or even with my more concentrated holdings. It is the years and decades of steady, consistent stock buying that will change my life, and can change yours.

Q: Is There Any Difference in How I Should Invest Based on My Age?

Of course, each person's financial background, investment time horizon, income, and life stage are different, but here are a few general ideas of what you could do with the Stock Planting ™ system in various decades of your life. Please note that these are broad generalizations I've come up with, everyone's situation is unique.

Ages 18-29:

One of my favorite ideas for this age group comes from Dave Ramsey, I really love what he says about this phase of life. I'm paraphrasing, but he says at this phase of life, the best investment you can make at this age is in YOU. What he means by that is your most powerful wealth building tool for your life is your income, and your ability to transform that monthly and yearly income into wealth by consistently saving and investing. Working to increase that income early can really pay off later.

So, at this age, as much as he and I are proponents of long-term investing and building wealth, I must agree, investing in the stock market at these ages will not make as much sense until you are into your first career that permits you to begin investing regularly in a retirement account like a 401(k) or IRA, and a post-tax investment account. This will be a different path for everyone, and some will be ready to begin investing before others. Graduating high school, getting through college or trade school if applicable, getting degrees, licenses, certifications etc. within a chosen work field with as little consumer debt as possible, will allow you to transform your income more quickly into wealth soon after, with more of your monthly dollars being able to go into investing accounts, instead of repaying costly debt.

Why not invest right away? We are all fans of compound interest, and the thought of investing as a teenager in a retirement account and letting it grow for 50 years is exciting, but I would still be hesitant due to all the typical uncertainty at this age. I know everyone's path is different, but here are a few examples. There may be lots of moving around at this age, deciding on a career path, likely changing that career path decision a few times, possibly buying or replacing a car, maybe moving again, possibly getting married, or possibly having children. These are just some examples of the expected life volatility typical of a person in their 20's and into their 30's.

So as boring as it sounds, and as much FOMO as you may have, typically a good investment at this age until you get "settled" a bit into a career, is boring cash in a high yield savings account. Having this cash liquid aka available will give you the flexibility to better handle what life may throw at you during this phase of life. If you get settled quickly into a career with little or no consumer debt early on, by all means, get invested in that 401(k) or other retirement or investment accounts. Playing "defense" financially by avoiding as much debt as possible during this phase of life allows the "offense" power of higher monthly contributions and compound interest to get started working for you earlier. With cash in the bank it offers you more mobility, too. You can even take more risks early on in finding a better career by having that cash buffer and ability to walk away from bad jobs if needed, without having an inability to pay bills and feeling stuck in a job or career that isn't right for you.

Ages 30-50:

I know this is a huge age range. This phase of life will hopefully find you settled or somewhat settled in a career field. Maybe it is not the ideal job you want forever, but a career field that at least interests and engages you enough to help other people, and helps you pay the bills. Hopefully during this time you're contributing regularly to retirement and investment accounts, following your version of the Stock Planting™ system outlined above.

Utilizing the behavior principles from *The Next Millionaire Next Door* book and avoiding excessive lifestyle creep can help keep your savings rate as high as you're able to manage as your income hopefully rises over the decades and you excel in your career path. Instead of focusing on a specific savings rate, I like Nick Maggilulli's take on savings rate from his book, *Just Keep Buying*. He says to save as much as you can, in the various seasons of your life. This amount may change over the years, and that is okay.

Life will have ups and downs, careers and incomes may change, so you must be open to adapting. You can work at improving within your career by taking on tough projects, additional credentials, certificates, anything relevant that can help you stay or become cream of the crop. A fantastic book on this is Seth Godin's *Linchpin*, which isn't an investing book but an amazing book on how to make yourself valuable within an organization, whether you stay there a long time or not. Steadily investing during these decades of ages 30-50 in your retirement, post-tax, and investment accounts and in your kid's college accounts if applicable, can help build a great nest egg. If you're starting this journey late, remember that it's never too late to start, but expectations about how many years you need to work until retirement and what your income situation may look like when you do retire may need to be adjusted, everyone's situation is different.

Ages 51+

I know this again is a large range, many may need or want to work much later than their 50's, 60's, and 70's, but I'd rather define this age group by the event of no longer working. Some people choose to retire very early as with the FIRE group, others are forced to retire early due to health or other reasons, but as soon as you stop taking your last paycheck, that renewed bi-monthly or monthly infusion of cash into your investment accounts will stop.

I don't want to get into specific recommendations, but it is good to keep in mind that there are a variety of investment ideas to help reduce your overall risk before or once those monthly paychecks from work stop. One thing many don't grasp that is unless your portfolio is incredibly massive (hopefully we're all in that boat!), stock market volatility and risk will hurt you more than they did previously while you were working, as you likely have three things working against you now.

1. You don't have continued contributions to help shore up market losses, what you have is what you have, unless you go back to work.

2. You may need to start drawing income from your portfolio to live on in retirement, which whittles down your portfolio faster in market down years and reduces gains in market up years.

3. If large losses do occur in your investment accounts, you may not have decades of time to help your portfolio grow back to that level, without taking income from your portfolio to live on. You still have to pay bills in retirement no matter what the market's doing.

I heard once that the stock market movement is like stair steps up, and an elevator down. I know this is a general statement and each situation is different, but I believe younger investors don't take enough risk, and many retirees take too much, often with neither group realizing it.

When you're younger, you have more time to ride the big drops and continue investing back up the stairs; when you've stopped working, the elevator drops tend to hurt more than the stair steps help. You must start thinking not just how to keep adding to and modifying your portfolio each year as you did while working, but now you must think through how to draw income streams from your portfolio. If you're in this last age group reading this, interviewing several different financial retirement advisors to see if any of them are a fit with what you're looking for may (or may not) be a way for you to go; each investor's comfort level and situation is different.

The Takeaways: The Stock Planting ™ system can be utilized by individuals in all age brackets listed, but the percent that single stock account or accounts make up of their entire net worth should be dependent on each investors situation and comfort level. When you're young and starting out with your financial journey, play good defense at first, so that when you're young to middle age, you can play GREAT offense. This sets you up to determine how much defense you may need to play when you're older.

Q: Should I Try to Rotate My Investments by Sector, Based on Economic Changes?

Sector Rotation - trying to buy stocks of sectors of the market predicted to perform well by economic changes over the coming months, quarters, or year - is very hard to do. Often, by the time most investors get a feel for which stocks may do well with the shifting of the economy, they unknowingly start buying at or near the peak of the rotation, only to sell out after some losses to chase the next rising sector. Analysts love to give advice on what sectors might do well in varying economic environments, and while they are not always wrong, it is my view that most investors are late to find out and even later to make the right moves in time.

The real sector rotation, if there was one, happened weeks or months ago, and very few accurately predicted it. While there are of course those few (think successful hedge fund managers) that can do it consistently, the way I like to think about sector rotation is much simpler and would likely get scoffed at in sophisticated groups. If there is a sector or industry of the market you think will do well in the coming months, quarter, or year, instead of selling assets to buy into it, simply notch some of those stocks higher up on your watchlist and start some Seed positions (remember a single share or fractional share) in some of the industry companies as your monthly deposits come into your accounts.

Time will tell whether you "rotated" efficiently or not, but either way, you haven't sold any of your current good positions to get there. If the new company stocks purchased are quality companies in good sectors, they may perform well for you in the long term, even if you did time the sector entry poorly and they drop short-term.

Over enough time, and I've advocated from the start to have a diversified portfolio among many different sectors, you may be pleasantly surprised when some of your existing positions you've held for years suddenly catch a small wave, as they are caught up in the sector rotation crowd. You won't be sucked into the hype though, you'll stick with your Stock Planting ™ system. You'll rebuy the stocks only if they reach your rebuy minimums, stop buying once you've reached your contribution cutoff, and start trimming once they reach the top percentage you're comfortable having that position make up of your account.

The Takeaways: Investing is already hard. For most of us, chasing cyclical sector rotation buys and sells based on changes in the economy will be a losing strategy. Buy great companies across many sectors and enjoy the ride through the varying market cycles.

Q: What about Investing Internationally?

This book was written for an audience in the USA, mostly due to my limited knowledge of foreign markets and retirement account setups abroad, but I hope its principles and especially the Stock Planting ™ system can be applied in markets around the world. As to whether you should invest internationally, the short answer is, yes. There are many amazing people in incredible countries working very hard all over the world to innovate and improve each day. I do hold some positions in international companies, and like my US based companies, some have done great, and others poorly.

What holds me back from investing a larger percent of my portfolio in international stocks is simply my ignorance of the local and government laws, cultures, regulations, restrictions, business risks, and many more ignorance's I'm sure I have of how these companies interact and do business daily. With the Stock Planting ™ system, you can certainly add some great companies to your portfolio one share at a time like with your other single stocks after some research, or you could utilize an ETF to get access to many foreign companies for some international exposure in your portfolio.

The Takeaways: It is arrogant to believe only US-based companies' stock can appreciate well for you in your portfolio, adding international companies can be a great diversification move. However, take care investing internationally, as Thomas Phelps said in *100 to 1 in the Stock Market*, "when you invest internationally you exchange risks you know, for risks you don't know."

Q: What Happens if a Company I Own Shares in Gets Bought by Another Company?

If you see a massive spike in one of your holdings one day, one of the many reasons could be that the company is going to get acquired by another company. Acquisitions are one of the ways companies can grow and hope to continue to add shareholder value, and if you own a large number of stocks as may happen over time investing the Stock Planting ^{TM} way, this is bound to happen to you eventually. When you find out this merger or acquisition is going to happen, I want you to evaluate the new company as if it were the stock at the top of your watchlist, next ready to buy.

Go through many of the same financial, product, service, stock performance, leadership etc. analysis you may (or may not) do before purchasing a Seed single stock position. If you are excited by the new company and think it could be a great partnership between the old and new company, then perhaps stay along for the ride. If you're uncomfortable being a shareholder of the new company, and you would never consider this company on your watchlist if this wasn't forced upon you, then maybe it is time to sell and put your investing dollars to work elsewhere.

Each time this happens with any of your holdings, go through this evaluation so either you're glad you sold, or you're glad you stayed. Last, sometimes you don't have enough shares in the old company for your shares to be worth it for the new company to take you on as a shareholder, so they will force you to sell the share or shares you own. This can be in addition to some cash they may or may not give you as part of the acquisition, so the decision was made for you. In that case, shrug your shoulders and move on. So many aspects of investing are out of our control, take ownership of what you can control.

The Takeaways: You have selected each of your positions with varying degrees of care, don't let the decision be made for you if you don't want to be a shareholder of the new acquiring company. Some investors have seen great investment growth sticking with the new acquiring company, for others it has been a losing deal, so make the decision yours.

189

CHAPTER 13: THE CLOSE

I don't have everything figured out yet. I feel fortunate to have learned from many great investors and teachers through books and podcasts about investing and the importance of behavior, humility, time horizon, risk, reward, luck, and patience. You may have found what appear to be glaring flaws in my system. If so, please send me a message! I'd love to hear your thoughts. If you found the book helpful, please send that message as well, and pass it along to someone else who you think could benefit from what you've learned.

I hope that by reading this book you have become more comfortable with single stock investing and investing in general. The whole point of this book is to take away the fear of investing. While winning financially will look different to everyone, I am optimistic that the concepts of this book could help everyone get closer to reaching their financial goals.

To be successful, a longer time horizon of many years seems necessary in almost all cases, and a steady hand of sticking to your personalized system. Stocks almost never go straight up and to the right, there is so much zigging and zagging, massive leaps, and devastating falls. But time is on your side if you allow it to be. The longer your time horizon, the longer you can let good people within good companies continue to innovate and improve, giving their stocks a chance to provide you with great compounding returns along the way. Remember, the most important points are when you take the plunge and buy a stock, when you buy more of the stock, and when you eventually sell some or all of it. Everything in between is mostly noise.

How I Invest

In the final chapter of *The Psychology of Money* by Morgan Housel, he tells his readers how he invests his money. I thought it was a great and unique way to finish a book, so I'd like to emulate that here. I don't want to give you my specific allocation numbers, after all this book is all about building your own unique system, but I do want to leave you with some of the behaviors and actions I've taken as part of my own journey so you can see I try to practice what I've preached. Finally, I want to conclude with some example portfolios to help you visualize what setting up your own investing parameters might look like, as well as provide some additional reading and listening material from those quoted in these pages.

I feel very fortunate and have worked very hard for decades to get here. I don't have any debt other than a mortgage and stay out of consumer debt, which helps free up monthly cash flow for investing. When I started investing in my 20's, it was only buying mutual funds through my company 401(k) plan. After years of reading about investing I started very small and cautiously, with a tiny amount of my income each month going into a Roth IRA. It was good for me to start small to build confidence, no shame there. Looking back, I can laugh at myself at the next part! I bought all sorts of weird speculative stocks and ETFs, mostly knee-jerk reactions to not wanting to miss out on things I heard or read about online that would be the "next big thing." A little shame there! Most of these small bets turned out to be bad investments, but good lessons.

As time went on, I read more from a wider group of smart people, and slowly developed my own investing thesis, system, and this Stock Planting ™ framework I laid out, taking the best bits of wisdom from everyone. I learned more about tax qualification and which investments might make sense among different accounts. I slowly expanded my investing from ETFs to single stocks, again making many short-term mistakes at first.

I was frustrated about not understanding why stocks went up or down so drastically at times, but even more frustrated feeling completely out of control. I developed much of my system through trial and error and attempting to invest more logically than emotionally over time. I knew I couldn't trust my future emotional self as much as I'd like to admit, so I wanted to set up a system I could follow without succumbing to investing fear, panic, or greed.

As my confidence grew and my system started to actually make sense, I started investing more of my monthly investment income into my single stock Roth IRA account and less into my 401(k) plan. I opened that REIT Roth IRA that I told you about earlier, and I opened a non-qualified investment account to start building that bridge account, for whatever life may throw at me. I still invest a portion in my company 401(k) plan each month to get a little bit of company match. I invest some into my Roth IRAs, a little into my post-tax investing account, and a tiny amount into cryptocurrency each month. I follow the Stock Planting ™ system with the Roth IRAs, Non-Qualified account, and cryptocurrency. I buy a mix of Growth and Value stocks in both Roth and Non-Qualified, but lean toward Value stocks in the Roth, and more Growth stocks in my Non-Qualified account, to avoid unnecessary dividend taxes. I love single stocks and predominantly invest in those, but still utilize EFTs in sectors of the investing world where I feel absolutely lost at having any chance of determining good vs bad investments, and would like to buy a group of stocks, instead of just one.

I still get excited seeing one of my Growth or Value stocks make it above their rebuy minimums so I get to buy more of a winner, and then rebuy more later, and even more excited once it grows to the "let it go" phase. I am glad when I am "forced" to trim a stock, because it means I've had a stellar performer, and get to take some gains off the table and keep that position at my peak comfortable level. I am even excited when the markets are pessimistic and everyone else is selling off, because usually this means there are no companies above their rebuy minimum, so I get to add some new top stock or stocks to my Seed Phase from my ever-growing watchlist.

There are so many opportunities in amazing companies out there, and optimism seems contagious in great companies and great people. I hope you have learned some lessons about investing and how to build your own Stock Planting ™ system, and some lessons about yourself as an investor. I challenge you to give Stock Planting ™ a try, with those first 10 stocks over 6 months, to see if it is for you! I hope we can learn to build useful emotional guardrail systems in many aspects of our lives, to control what we can, and learn to let go of what we cannot control; this can have peaceful implications in our lives far beyond our stocks.

Example Portfolios

These example portfolios are examples only - numbers I pulled at random - there is not one that is better than the other, and my own allocation numbers are not right in the middle as some might guess, I just want to help you put pen to paper on your own Stock Planting ™, and these portfolios are ideas to get you thinking. For my audiobook listeners I will include an accompanying PDF. While I will read these numbers off, they are much easier to visualize together on a screen than in audio format.

Category	Investor A	Investor B
Number of stocks to start out with before adding shares to any existing positions	20	50
Minimum (rebuy) total percent gain reached in an existing position before adding more share(s) to that position for Value (dividend-paying) stocks, Growth (no dividend) stocks.	Value 15%, Growth 30%	Value 20%, Growth 50%
Time period a stock must maintain its gain above the rebuy minimum to be rebought	First available payday deposit	2-4 weeks
Target percent the position will make up of the total account after the first repurchase	Target: 10%	Target: 3%

Contribution Cutoff percent to any one position	25%	10%
Let it Ride Phase	25% - 50%	10% - 20%
Trimming Phase	50.1%	20.1%
Maximum Drawdown sell point for a single position	-80%	-60%
Holding Period	6 years	10 years

References and Recommendations:

I must give credit to the incredibly smart men and women I learned and continue to learn from. I mentioned each of them only briefly and some weren't specifically included in the book but contributed to my learning. I recommend each of these books and podcasts as timeless reads, re-reads, and great listens. If you find more books that you think I should add, please let me know!

Books (alphabetical order)

100 to 1 in the Stock Market – Thomas W Phelps

100 Baggers - Christopher W. Mayer

Antifragile - Nassim Nicholas Taleb

Dividend Growth Investing - Freeman Publications

Ego is the Enemy - Ryan Holliday

Just Keep Buying - Nick Maggiulli

Linchpin - Seth Godin

Money: Master the Game - Tony Robbins

Nothing but Net - Mark Mahaney

The Motley Fool Million Dollar Portfolio - David Gardner, Tom Gardner

The Next Millionaire Next Door - Sarah Stanley Fallaw, Thomas J Stanley

One-up on Wall Street - Peter Lynch

The Psychology of Money - Morgan Housel

REIT Investing for Beginners – Freeman Publications

Stocks for the Long Run - Jeremy Siegel

The Titanium Economy - Asutosh Padhi, Gaurav Batra, Nick Santhanam

The Total Money Makeover - Dave Ramsey

Why Does the Stock Market Go Up? - Brian Feroldi

Podcasts (Alphabetical Order)

Animal Spirits

Bankless

Choose FI

Motley Fool Money

Rule Breaker Investing

The Tape

Trillions

The Best One Yet

What Goes Up